# THE DEADLY DECEPTION

by **James D. Shaw**
*33rd Degree, Knight Commander of the Court of Honor,*
*Past Worshipful Master, Blue Lodge, Past Master of*
*All Scottish Rite Bodies,*
and
**Tom C. McKenney**

# DEDICATION

*To the multitudes of sincere men seeking Light.*

## ACKNOWLEDGMENTS

My humble thanks to all the friends who have assisted and encouraged me, especially Gynel Newton Wilson, Jackson, Tennessee, who generously gave hundreds of hours in coordinating preparation of the manuscript, and whose consistent encouragement was salted with sound editorial advice.

**Huntington House, Inc.**
P.O. Box 53788, Lafayette, Louisiana 70505

Library of Congress Catalog Card Number 88-081728
ISBN Number 0-910311-52-8

Printed in the United States of America

# TABLE OF CONTENTS

# FOREWORD

Freemasonry, *sincerely* entered into, is a search for light. Any knowledgeable Mason can tell you this. Yet, beneath the surface of this search for light, there is much more. This truth is seldom realized by the Masonic candidate. As a matter of fact, the vast majority of Masonic seekers are never aware that there *is* anything more available to them in Masonry, beyond what they see and hear in their Blue Lodge experience. Quite naturally, they settle for that.

Yet the very richness of meaning in the word "light" should tell us that in the light they seek there should be truth — answers to deep questions. There should come revelations of the meaning of life, death and eternal things.

Very few Masons realize this and press on through the degrees and offices of Masonry and the writings of the Masonic philosophers in an unending search for enlightenment — for intellectual and spiritual fulfillment.

Only a small number make that extra commitment that goes far beyond social and business motivations. They continue to work, study, seek and learn, climbing the mountain of Masonic knowledge, searching for that light in all its fullness.

Jim Shaw was such a man. He was not satisfied with social fulfillment or surface knowledge; he sensed the deeper, true meaning of that promised light and he sought it with all his heart, mind and strength. His ardent quest carried him through all the chairs of leadership in the Blue Lodge and the Scottish Rite, all the way to the House of the Temple in Washington, D.C. to the "Thirty-Third and Last Degree" and the position of Sovereign Grand Inspector General, Knight Commander of the House of the Temple of Solomon. There, at the top of the Masonic mountain, he broke through the clouds at last and found the full revelation, the true meaning of light and life. This is his story. Come and make that pilgrimage to Truth with him.

**Tom C. McKenney**
*Marion, Kentucky*

# Chapter 1

# ON MY OWN

My mother married for the second time when I was two years old. I was, of course, too young to understand that my father had deserted us when I was only a few months old. I have never seen him.

As time passed, my stepfather developed a growing dislike for me that I accepted as normal, having no knowledge or experience against which to judge life. He really loved my mother, I think, in his own imperfect way. But his resentment of me created problems for her almost from the start.

My Christian grandmother was a beloved and powerful influence in my life. She loved me. Our mutual love and her obvious dislike of my stepfather contributed to his ever-increasing hatred and rejection of me.

However my origin, my grandmother and our love for one another impacted on my problems at home, these took a giant leap for the worse with the birth of my little half-sister. It was only natural that my stepfather would favor her, which he definitely and obviously did. If there was anything remaining of our father-son relationship, it vanished with her coming.

After my little sister, three boys were born. With the coming of each one, my stepfather's life was increasingly fulfilled with his own babies. Simultaneously, I grew older, losing any "little boy" advantage with which I may have begun our relationship. I just became, obviously and completely, an unwanted, adolescent ugly duckling, an entirely unwelcome complication in his home.

**9**

## WORK BEGINS EARLY

Unpleasant as all this was for me, I accepted it. I had never known anything else. And I was busy. My stepfather had decreed I must work and support myself. So I did, beginning with my first newspaper route at age five. Soon I was buying all my own clothes, books and school supplies.

During elementary school I had a newspaper route which I delivered early in the morning before going to school and a second job working in the neighborhood drugstore after school. In the evenings I walked, doing my paper route collections, and selling extra papers up and down the streets. I kept up with my school work, worked at my jobs and stayed out of trouble — except at home.

## LIVING WITH PHYSICAL ABUSE

Things really didn't seem so bad. I just did what I had to do and thought my life was fairly normal—except for one thing. The beatings I took from my stepfather didn't seem normal to me. They were frequent, whenever he could find the slightest excuse—and they were nothing like the loving chastening a godly father should give his child. They were beatings. But I took them, not seeing any alternative, and made the best of things. I could cling to the belief that my mother and grandmother loved me. This was my life through the age of 12.

## THE BEATINGS COME TO AN END

I was 13 the day I saw my stepfather hit my mother with his fist. I didn't take time to think . I just reacted in a reflex built way down deep inside my very nature. I jumped him, pulled him away from her, and a wild fight followed. Although he was much larger than I, and I was only a boy, I fought with the fury of a son rescuing his beloved mother, and with the pent-up anger of a lifetime of physical and emotional abuse. I fought him to the floor. He got up and left the house. Although I didn't realize it, this part of my life had come to an end.

## "YOU MUST GO"

The next afternoon, when I came home from working at the drugstore, my mother was waiting for me in the front yard. She was crying. She stopped me short of the house and said, "Jimmie, Joe says you must pack up and leave. He says he can't stand having you around here anymore, and you must go."

She was choking on the words. And as the reality of what I was hearing came into focus in my mind, weeping rose up within me and spilled over. We wept there, standing in the front yard, but this was something we both had to face. She now had four younger children besides me and a life she had to live.

## The seed is planted

As I shouldered my school books and what little clothing I had, my mother went on to say, "Now, Jimmie, I want you to get a room near your work; and since you have been supporting yourself anyway, maybe it won't be too difficult for you. Jimmie, I want you to try to be a man. Try to be like your Uncle Irvin (her brother); he is a good man and a Mason. He goes to church and is good to his family and if you get to know him better maybe you can grow up to be a good man and a Mason like he is."

My mother knew nothing of what Freemasonry is but she knew her brother as a hard-working, church-going, good man.

My stepfather had forbidden that anyone in our family attend church services, saying that all the people in the churches were hypocrites. I believe that the fact that Uncle Irvin was an active member of the Methodist Church was the main reason my mother looked up to him. She wanted me to be like him. The seed that would later germinate, spring up, and grow to full fruit in ardent commitment to Freemasonry, taking me to its high levels of service and leadership, was planted.

Although I didn't realize it then, the course of much of my life already was set. But I wouldn't just become a good Mason like my Uncle Irvin; I would go far beyond him in the Craft, far, far beyond him, for it would become the center of knowledge, wisdom and religious fulfillment in my life.

My life would come to be built around my search for light and the fellowship I found in the Masonic Order and its various bodies.

As we stood there in the front yard that pivotal, painful day she went on to advise me. "Stay out of pool rooms," she said, and I always have. "Don't smoke cigarettes," she said, and I never have.

She added, "If you must smoke, smoke cigars like your Uncle Irvin;" and for many years of my life, I did.

As she spoke, I began to realize the enormity of what was happening. With this realization growing within me and blinded with tears, I reached out to her, hugged her, turned and walked away. As I took each step up the street and away from mother, the weight of the world and of an unknown future settled down on my 13-year-old shoulders.

I was on my own.

# Chapter 2

# IN SEARCH
# OF A
# FUTURE

The first thing I had to do after leaving home and my mother —
now on my own for the first time in my life — was to find a place
to live. Mother had suggested that I find a room near my work and
I did, at a rooming house just down the street from the drugstore.
The owner of the drugstore gave me longer hours to work so that
I could give up the paper route. I began to adjust to my new life.

Working in the drugstore, going to school and studying filled my
days and nights. But I was able to keep up with my school work and
in this way finished elementary school and high school, including
four years of ROTC[1].

During those first years on my own, my grandmother was even
more important in my life. She was a real rock of stability and
support and we became very close.

She tried to get Uncle Irvin to take me places and spend time with
me because she knew I had never known a father. She wanted him
to help fill that void in this growing boy's relatively empty life and
I very much wanted that. But he was too busy — always too busy
— with his Masonic Lodge activities, his work at the post office
and his own family.

Mother had set him up as my father figure and role model, and I really wanted to know him; but he was too busy.

## ALONE AGAIN

After high school graduation, with the encouragement and financial support of my grandmother, I began the study of law. In those days it was possible to enter the study of law directly out of high school, earn the LLB[2] degree from the state university and take the bar examination. But after only one year my grandmother died and I was forced to drop out of law school. My world suddenly became much more empty. My one real friend and supporter on earth was gone. I was alone again.

## BONNIE ENTERS MY LIFE

But my work kept me busy, and I got an additional job that summer, hoping that maybe I could earn enough money for another year of law school. By this time I was definitely interested in girls and, although there was precious little time for them, I began to meet some and get to know them. That summer I met Bonnie and almost everything in my life changed! It was another turning point. But, as usual, I didn't realize it at the time.

Bonnie was wonderful. She seemed to return this sentiment and her family liked and approved of me. Things developed quickly, we decided to marry and soon did. Since my second job (in hopes of another year of law school) was in a restaurant and I was learning a good deal about the restaurant business, Bonnie's family suggested that we go into that business. They lent us the money to buy a place that was for sale. We cleaned, painted and decorated it nicely and were soon doing a good business. We were enjoying the work, prospering and were quite happy with it all, and with each other. Life was good.

Law school was disappearing on the road behind me now. The path of my life had taken a permanent turn in another direction.

## MY FIRST EXPERIENCE OF FRATERNAL ORDERS

One day a man who was eating in our restaurant asked to see me. I went over to the side table where he was seated and asked him what he wanted. He said he was a representative of the Loyal Order of the Moose and that I had been selected to be a member. He also said that it would provide important social and business contacts and would be good for my restaurant business.

It sounded good to me and before long I was a member. At the same time, Bonnie joined the Women of the Moose. It was the beginning of our active involvement in fraternal orders and I had not the slightest idea of where it would eventually take me.

The Moose Lodge was quite different from the Masonic orders I would later know so well. For one thing, the Moose meetings were quite short. Our lodge met upstairs over a lunchroom and bar. When the relatively short meetings were over, nearly everyone went downstairs to the bar where things continued for a much longer time (sometimes it almost seemed that this was the real reason for meeting).

Still, I didn't attend the Moose meetings very often until I was approached about being an officer. Now, for the boy who had never felt accepted and had never been an officer in anything, this was pretty heady stuff; I immediately accepted, necessarily becoming much more active.

The lunchroom under the Lodge Hall belonged to the Lodge. The man who operated the business had to pay no rent, nor did he have any utility costs, which made his brisk business even more profitable. He was a member of the Lodge and I envied his advantage in business, compared with my own situation.

## MOTHER'S LAST GOODBYE

In all the time that Bonnie and I had operated the restaurant, Uncle Irvin had never been there, so I was surprised one day to see him coming in. He said that my grandfather was outside in the car but didn't feel well enough to come inside. I went out to the car to see him and could see at a glance that grandfather was very, very sick and weak. We visited briefly and then Uncle Irvin drove away. It was the last time I saw grandfather alive; he died the following week.

At his funeral, I noticed that mother did not look well at all. She appeared pale and weak, struggling, it seemed, just to sit up. I had never seen her look so ill, but I thought it was just the pain and stress of losing her father. I didn't feel free to stay very close to her, since my stepfather was there. But I comforted her as best I could and, as we parted, she told me goodbye. How could I have suspected that it was her last goodbye? The following week she died, and the following Saturday, exactly one week after grandfather's funeral, we buried mother.

I have never been able to find out what caused her death. Even to this day, there is something mysterious about it as if something is being concealed; but it seems to have been a heart attack.

After the funeral service was completed, my stepfather came over to where Bonnie and I were standing and said, "Jim, I feel that I need to tell you something. I believe that your mother would still be alive had it not been for the way I treated you."

Then he said, emotionally, "I will never marry again!" Six months later he was remarried. But I do believe there was truth in what he told me about mother's death. He was never again any part of my life.

## WAR COMES

Not long after mother's death, the Great War came and ended the Great Depression. The Japanese bombed Pearl Harbor and America entered the conflict. We were in it at last and the operator of the lunchroom at the Moose Lodge was drafted. This opened up that position and the governing board asked me to take it over. Bonnie and I talked it over and decided I would probably also be drafted soon, so we sold our restaurant (in order to be ready) and were soon working full time at the Moose Lodge. Our lives were even more closely tied to fraternal orders now. Still we had no idea where it would lead.

More than a year went by. I tried to join the Navy but was turned down. We stayed busy with the lunchroom and lodge activities. I had really forgotten about the draft when the notice came. I had been drafted.

## THE MASONIC CONNECTION

I had been out of high school more than six years and married for five years when I entered the Army during World War II. Yet from the very first I began to remember what my mother had said to me, that awful day at age 13 when I had been forced to leave home.

Maybe it was because, once again, I was alone and entering into an unknown way of life. I remembered about my Uncle Irvin and his active involvement in the Masonic Lodge. As I went through basic training I noticed that many of the officers there wore Masonic rings.

Toward the end of basic training, two men from my unit were to be selected for Officer Candidate School to be trained as officers and commissioned second lieutenants. I was not selected and the two who were selected were both Masons. I thought about my four years of ROTC, my age, my experience and wondered why I had not been selected. I didn't realize then that these men had been selected by Masons because they were Masons. In later years I would understand very well . But at the time I could only wonder.

## CLIMBING "SHAW HILL"

I was much older than the other men in my company. As a matter of fact, I was older than my company commander. In spite of my "advanced age," I had been assigned to the infantry, and was baseplate man in the mortar platoon of a rifle company. We traveled on foot and I had the heaviest load to carry. The others called me "Pop," but I didn't mind. I carried my baseplate, plus my own weapon and all my individual gear, and usually outdid the younger men.

As a matter of fact, during a training march from Camp Butner to Raleigh, North Carolina, I was the only man in the company able to carry another man to the top of a certain hill along the way.

My platoon commander congratulated me, named it "Shaw Hill," and that little honor meant a lot more to me than anyone else there could have known. I still think at times of that hill, about halfway between Camp Butner and Raleigh, and what Lieutenant Ram said that day about this abandoned little kid from the big city.

The war came and went and, with that behind me, I was even more sure that I could make it in life. With Bonnie at my side, I knew that I could succeed. Mother would be pleased if she knew. I *really could* be a successful, good man like my Uncle Irvin.

## Footnotes

[1] *Reserve Officer Training Corps, a training program that prepares young men to be officers in the Army. High School ROTC prepares the men for college ROTC, and that leads to a commission as second lieutenant.*
[2] *Bachelor of Laws and Letters, the traditional law school degree.*

# Chapter 3

# BROUGHT TO THE LIGHT

The war was over and I was home again with Bonnie. We were supremely happy — and together we were about to enter into the Masonic fellowship that would become our world.

I soon told Bonnie that I would really like to join the Masonic Lodge. I remembered the Masonic officers in basic training and I had a need to belong, a need for acceptance in a group, for friends, for a family.

Immediately I received a surprising revelation from Bonnie: she had been a member of the Order of the Eastern Star since age 18, and her father was a Mason! I was amazed; I had no idea of any of this. She had never attended a meeting or even mentioned it to me since I had known her. But she was happy that I wanted to be a Mason.

I was happy that we already had this little foundation laid, and now I earnestly pursued the idea.

## WHY ALL THESE PENNIES ?

I was still a member in good standing in the Moose Lodge. During the war, while I had been away, my dues had been suspended (it was the patriotic thing to do). We had many good friends in the Moose Lodge, I was made welcome there and it was as if I had never been away — except that we no longer operated the lunchroom.

I told a few friends in the Moose that I was thinking of joining the Masonic Lodge and discovered that there was no conflict at all. Three of my Moose brothers were also Masons. They were pleased that I wanted to be one too.

Each one of them gave me a penny and told me to "keep it handy," as I would be needing it.

They were a bit mysterious about it and didn't explain, so I wondered what all this penny business was about but didn't ask. I wondered even more as days passed, because every Mason I mentioned this to did the same thing! I soon had quite a few pennies and was certain that it was important to "keep it handy," but hadn't the slightest idea why. Then, the mysterious nature of Masonry was one of the things about it that attracted me. I began to look forward to entering in with increased anticipation.

As the Christmas season approached in late 1945 I found a temporary job at the post offiice. Uncle Irvin was assistant postmaster and could have helped me to get the job, but he didn't. I got the job without his help, was working the second shift, and we were getting along fine.

## FIRST STEPS TOWARD THE LIGHT

Bonnie and I had two close friends, Mac and Merle, whom we had known before the war. Merle had worked for us at the restaurant and had later married Mac. One evening they invited us over to their home and, after dinner, when the ladies were in the kitchen, I asked Mac (who was a Mason) how I could get into the Masonic Lodge.

He was delighted, and replied, "All you have to do is ask. I will get a friend of mine at the Fire Department to recommend you, and with my recommend[1] that will get the ball rolling."

About two weeks passed and I had a phone call from a man who said he was on the Masonic Lodge committee that would be talking with me and asked if they might come over that evening.

I told him I would be glad for them to come and after dinner that evening, three men[2] came. We visited and they asked me questions about myself, including my reasons for wanting to join. They were pleasant, and Mac had already told me what to expect so I was at ease throughout the interview. They left in agreement that I would be taken into the Lodge.

## PREPARATION FOR INITIATION

A few days later I received a letter telling me to be at the Lodge Hall at 7 p.m. Tuesday evening. I arrived promptly and found that two others were to be initiated along with me.

We were met by the Lodge secretary who told us what the cost of the initiation would be and explained that these dues (fees that must be paid) would have to be paid for all three degrees before we could proceed with the first degree initiation.

I paid my dues and, when the others had settled their business, we were taken to a room which I later knew very well as the "Preparation Room." But at the time I had no idea where I was or why I was there. In the Preparation Room we were told to remove all clothing, and were then given a two-piece garment made of thin, white material that looked like pajamas; and we were given one sandal each. We were told to put the sandal on the right foot, leaving the left foot bare. We were now prepared to receive the Entered Apprentice Degree, or the First Degree in Freemasonry.

A man called "The Senior Deacon" then entered and asked questions of us such as "Why do you wish to become Freemasons; do you join because you believe it will help you in your business, or help you to gain influence in your community?"

Now, to such questions the candidate is supposed to answer as if he had no such selfish motivation. But it has been my experience that the vast majority of Masons enter for these very self-serving reasons. As a matter of fact, although the theory is that Masons do not recruit, or advise prospects that there are business and professional advantages in being a Mason, both are commonly done. Again, Mac had prepared me by warning me about such questions and I gave satisfactory answers. But I was able to do so honestly, for I really did have an earnest desire to join and to belong — just to belong. Then the Senior Deacon left.

After the departure of the Senior Deacon, I was blindfolded. The blindfold is called a "hoodwink," and the candidate so prepared is said to be "hoodwinked," unable to see or know the truth of his surroundings or situation.

After the hoodwink was placed over my eyes, a heavy cloth was further placed under it and over my eyes to insure that I would not be able to see anything, not even a crack of light.

Then the light cloth shirt was arranged so that my left arm was out of it, and the left side of the shirt folded back and tucked under, leaving the left arm and left side of the torso bare. The left leg of the "pajama bottoms" was rolled up high, leaving the left foot and leg bare. A blue rope (called a "cabletow") was tied around my neck. I was ready.

Although I very much wanted to be taken into the Masonic Lodge, I began to experience real fear. I couldn't see, didn't know where I was, was half-naked among an unknown number of strangers, being held by a rope around my neck, and I certainly didn't know what would happen next. There was a sense of unreality and helplessness and a rising groundswell of disorientation, insecurity and fear. Mac had told me (although he was under a terrible oath not to do so) a little of what to expect. I knew I would be blindfolded but expected to be able to see a little bit anyway. However, I could see nothing at all.

This being in total darkness produced a deep-down feeling of helplessness, and gave rise to thoughts of terrible things that might be done. The thing that kept me from being overwhelmed with fear was the knowledge that Mac, Uncle Irvin and my Masonic friends in the Moose Lodge were all alive and well. Since they all had somehow survived this, I believed that I would survive it too. But I was extremely uncomfortable.

## INTO THE HOLY PLACE

The Steward led me to the Lodge Hall door and instructed me to give three raps. Nothing happened at first and then there were three answering raps from inside and a voice asked, "Who comes here?"

The Steward, answering for me, replied, "A poor blind candidate who desires to be brought from darkness into light, and receiving a part of the rights, lights and benefits of this Worshipful Lodge dedicated to the Holy Saints John, as many a brother and fellow have done before him."

I was asked, "Is this an act of your own free will and accord?" Prompted by the Steward, I replied, "It is."

It was already becoming apparent to me that, although I really wanted to be a Mason, this was not to be an honest exchange between me and these unseen persons; there were prearranged "right" answers to all their prearranged questions, and I would be told how to reply. The voice on the other side of the door asked if I were properly prepared and worthy and well-qualified. To both questions the Steward replied in the affirmative.

Then the other voice asked, "By what further right or benefit does he expect to gain admission?"

The Steward replied, for me, "By being a man, free born, of lawful age and well-recommended."[3]

The voice on the other side then said, "Let him wait with patience until the Worshipful Master is informed and his answer returned."

After another period of waiting in the black silence the door was opened before me and the voice said that I was to be allowed to enter and be received "in due and ancient form." I was led through the door. Although I didn't know where I was, I had passed through the protected portals and into the holy and secret place. I was inside a Lodge Hall for the first time in my life.

## BROUGHT TO THE LIGHT

That same voice I heard from inside the door (it turned out to be the Senior Deacon) then said, from directly in front of me, "You are received into this Lodge of Entered Apprentices upon the point of a sharp instrument piercing your naked left breast, which is to teach you as this is an instrument of torture to the flesh, so the remembrance of it be to your mind and conscience, should you ever presume to reveal any of the secrets of Freemasonry unlawfully."

The "sharp instrument" was actually a large compass with the two sharp points brought together as one, and "sharp" it most certainly was. I *really did* feel pain as it was pressed into my flesh. When he said "presume," he emphasized the word by jabbing me again. This thing was becoming more and more serious and I was even more afraid. Yet, under the circumstances, I stood silently and made no reply.

I was then caused to walk again, led by the same man who was holding me by the rope around my neck and by my left arm. We stopped. Another voice (it was the Worshipful Master) ordered me taken to a place in the center of the room for prayer. I was led there, made to kneel, and the Master prayed a formal, generalized prayer, never mentioning Jesus, and ending with, "So mote it be."

After the prayer he came to where I was kneeling, placed his hand on my head and asked, "In whom do you place your trust?"

Except for the few times as a child with my grandmother I had not been taken to church or taught about God and I really didn't know how to reply. I was awkwardly silent for what seemed a long time.

Finally the Senior Deacon leaned over and whispered in my ear that I should say "In God,"[4] and I did. The Master then said that since my trust was in God my faith was well-founded and I was to follow my "conductor" (the Senior Deacon, who was leading me around by the rope around my neck) and not be afraid. That helped a little but I was still far from being at ease.

I was then led to another place in the room where another man (the Junior Warden) asked the same questions as before my being allowed to enter the room. He then directed me to be led to still another place where the Senior Warden asked the very same questions and received the same replies. At each stop someone rapped once with a gavel.

It was all very strange and formal and the questions and answers were beginning to sound familiar. From there I was led to the position of "the Worshipful Master in the East" where he asked the *very same* questions and received the very same replies. It was really beginning to be repetitious. Then, at the direction of the Worshipful Master, I was instructed in the proper manner of "approaching the East."[5] The Senior Deacon, my principal escort, turned me around saying, "You will face the East. Take one step with your left foot, and bring the heel of your right foot to the hollow (instep) of your left foot, feet forming the angle of the oblong square."

He helped me do this because I could not see. He held on to me or I might have lost my balance. It was an unnatural way to stand and being blindfolded made it even more difficult. Then, suddenly, he shouted, "STAND ERECT!"[6]

I was startled and wondered what *that* was all about (I was already standing up, although my feet were somewhat twisted around). But I was beginning to expect such unexpected things and, although I certainly didn't know it, an even more startling surprise was just ahead.

The voice of the Worshipful Master, somewhere in front of me, said, "Friend, for the first time in your life you have advanced to the altar of Masonry; you stand before us a candidate seeking admission to our Order. But before going farther be warned of the solemnity and importance of the step you are about to take. If you are unwilling to proceed, withdraw while there is yet time."

There had been moments of fear when I wanted to leave, but felt trapped in what was taking place. And now, as I awkwardly stood there, blindfolded and disoriented, not knowing what (or how many) men may be looking at me, I began to feel a strange kind of numbness. I felt somewhat like a victim still, but really didn't want to leave. I was beginning to feel as if I were being carried along, propelled by a force I neither knew nor understood. The Master went on with remarks about the nature of the Order and of the high moral character required to belong.

Then I was placed in a kneeling position before the altar, "in due form." This was to kneel on the naked left knee, right leg extended to form the Tau Cross ("angle of a square"), left hand under the Bible on the altar (on top of which were the square and compass), right hand resting thereon and body erect. I was now ready to take the oath, although I certainly didn't know it, and I knew *nothing* of what would be *in* that oath.

## KISSING JESUS GOODBYE

The Master then assured me that the oath which I was about to take would in no way "conflict with religious, political or private pursuits be they what they may,"[7] and, asked me if I were willing to continue. I really didn't know what he was talking about but it sounded reassuring so I said, "I am."

I was then led to swear, repeating after the Worshipful Master, the oath of an Entered Apprentice Mason. He would speak a few words and I would repeat them, having no idea to what I was swearing until each small group of words was spoken for me to repeat.

As it progressed I realized that I was swearing to protect the secrets of the Lodge. Then I heard myself saying that I was "binding myself under no less penalty than that of having my throat cut from ear to ear, my tongue torn out by its roots, and buried in the sands of the sea a cable's length from shore, where the tide ebbs and flows twice in twenty-four hours, should I ever willingly, knowingly, or unlawfully violate this, my Entered Apprentice Oath, so help me God and keep me steadfast."

The awfulness of the oath dawned within me as I was speaking it and it was both frightening and repulsive to me. But, having begun, having "come this far," I just continued to the end.[8] The Master then told me that, in order to seal this oath, I was to kiss the open Bible before me. I had my hands on it so I knew where it was and I leaned forward and kissed it. I had no idea that I was actually kissing Jesus goodbye at a pagan altar. I didn't know that throughout my lifetime in Masonry I would not be allowed to pray in His name, or even to hear or speak His name in the Lodge, even in Scripture readings.[9] But I didn't know Him then, so would have had no sense of loss even had I known this.

## I WANTED A GLASS OF WATER

The Worshipful master then directed that since I was now bound to the Lodge "by an oath which cannot be broken," I was to have the rope (cabletow) removed from my neck.

The Senior Deacon removed it.

Then the Master said to me, "My brother, in your present blind condition, what do you most desire?"

Well, I had been through a lot of stress by that time and was very thirsty. I assumed from his question that whatever I asked for, I would probably be given. So I thought it over briefly and was just about to say, "a cold glass of water," when the Senior Deacon leaned over and whispered in my ear, "Light."

So, a little disappointed, I said, "Light."

The big surprise was just about ready. The Master called the lodge members to the altar and they gathered in two rows, one on either side of me, aligned east-to-west.

He then quoted from Genesis where God said, "Let there be light" and said, "In solemn imitation of Him I, in like manner, Masonically declare, 'let there be LIGHT!' "

When he shouted "LIGHT" all the other men present around me clapped their hands and stamped their feet simultaneously, startling me half to death and, at the same moment, the Senior Deacon ripped off the hoodwink and I was blinded with brilliant light.

The Worshipful Master then said, "And there is light."

I was stunned and dazzled momentarily. Then the Master went on talking, explaining the objects I was beginning to be able to focus my eyes on and see before me. He told me about the Bible,[10] square, and compass, their meaning, and called them the "three great lights of Masonry." Then he referred to the three candles around the altar and said they represented the "three lesser lights" of Masonry, which in reality are the sun, the moon, and the Worshipful Master of the Lodge. None of this meant much to me at that time, except that I already had a vague idea that the Bible was supposed to be a sacred book.

Then the Worshipful Master showed me how to perform the due-guard (by holding my hands in the position in which they had been at the altar, left one palm-up and the right one over it, palm-down), and the sign. The sign was performed by drawing the open hand from the left ear, across the throat to the right ear, as if cutting the throat across. I was still kneeling at the altar. The Master then demonstrated the secret grip (pressing the knuckle of the right index finger) and gave me the secret word, ("Boaz").

He helped me to stand and instructed me to go and salute the Junior and Senior Wardens with the due-guard and sign. Led by the Senior Deacon, I did.

Returning then to the west side of the altar, I waited while the

Master approached the altar and presented me with a lambskin apron. He explained that it was an emblem of innocence and the mark of a Mason. He further spoke of its importance and then told me to take it to the Senior Warden in the West who would instruct me in the way to wear it. I did it, thinking that there is a very great deal of moving around in these ceremonies.

The Senior Warden explained its use by ancient stonemasons and by members of the Lodge, or "speculative" Masons, including the way I should wear it (with the bib turned up). Then he put the apron on me, led me back to my place at the altar, we both saluted the Worshipful Master and he reported, "Your orders have been obeyed, Worshipful Master."

## The Pennies Explained

At this point the Master asked me to deposit something of value of a metallic kind and directed me to search my person for such an object.

"The pennies," I thought, "this is what the pennies were about."

Well, I knew there was no use looking in those pajamas for a coin for they had no pockets. The Master then explained that all this was to remind me of my "poor and penniless condition," should I ever meet a friend, particularly a brother Mason, who is destitute. I was to give to him, as able to do so "without inconvenience."

Then I was sent to the preparation room to dress again and then return for further instruction.

I went, thinking, "This explains all that mysterious stuff about the pennies, and yet it doesn't. They said I would be *needing* them and I really don't."

It was a partial truth — but not the clear, plain truth. I had actually been misled. I wondered if somehow this was an indication of deceptions to come. I had believed them completely and it had really not been true.

Upon my return, I saluted the Worshipful Master and was seated as a member of the Lodge. I watched, with growing understanding, as the other two candidates were initiated after me.

I was a Mason at last — without any help from Uncle Irvin.

## Footnotes

[1] A recommendation for acceptance is called a "recommend" in the Lodge, as is the case with Mormons seeking admission to the secret rituals of the Mormon Temple. Joseph Smith, founder of Mormonism and writer of the temple ritual, was a Mason. Much of the Mormon Temple ritual is the same as in Masonic ritual, having apparently been "borrowed" from it by Smith. Two such "recommends" are required before admission to the Masonic Lodge can be pursued.

[2] These three men constituted the "Investigation Committee"; there are always three men, and they are elected each year to this position.

[3] Although essentially the same, the rituals for the first three ("Blue") degrees vary in small ways from state to state in the USA. In most states the wording here includes "white," for Negroes and women are entirely excluded from the Masonic brotherhood. There is a Negro Masonic system, called the Prince Hall Lodge, but it is not associated in any way with "white" Freemasonry. It is referred to as "clandestine" Masonry, and is considered by the rest of Masonry to be a spurious, illegitimate imitation.

[4] Some really funny things do happen in these ceremonies. Once, later on, when I was Worshipful Master, I placed my hand on a candidate's head and asked him, "In whom do you place your trust?" Without hesitation the man replied, "My wife."

[5] "The east" is the location within the Lodge Hall where the Worshipful Master sits upon his throne/chair of authority. In the ancient mystery religions, from which Freemasonry springs, the Sun was worshipped, and the most sacred direction was east, where the sun arose each morning to renew life on earth.

[6] This position of the feet is no coincidence when facing the Worshipful Master "in the East." This position of the feet forms the "Tau Cross," a phallic symbol from antiquity associated with phallic worship and Sun worship in which the Sun was viewed as the source of life (male), rising each day in the east to impregnate the Earth (female) with new life. Such worship was always done facing East. Here in the ritual, the command "STAND ERECT" is also not a coincidence, and is of obvious symbolic meaning. See Appendix B, "Masonic Symbolism."

[7] This is, at best, logically absurd. He could have no way of knowing this, for he had no knowledge of what such values, beliefs and standards I may have held, then or in the future. One clear exception to this false assurance, for example, is that all Christians are forbidden by Scripture from taking such oaths, particularly blood oaths of mayhem and murder.

[8] There have been cases reported of men who stopped at the point of the terrible oath and refused to continue, but such cases are rare. By the time most men are at this point, nearly finished with the oath, they will, because of fear, their humbling position, the rope around the neck, and the hypnotic effect of the ceremony, proceed with the oath, although they may feel revulsion at it.

[9] In a "well-ordered Lodge" the name of Jesus is not allowed to be spoken. Praying in His name is a serious offense and can even bring about the closing of

*a lodge. When New Testament Scriptures are read in the rituals, portions including the name of Jesus are simply omitted.*

[10] *In this part of the ritual the Worshipful Master tells the initiate," the Holy Bible is to be your rule and guide to your faith and practice." Years later, when I was a Worshipful Master, a friend who was an officer in the Lodge asked me, after an initiation, "Jim, if it is true that the Bible is to be our rule and guide, why don't we follow its teachings?" He had an excellent question, one for which I had no answer, and he soon left Masonry.*

# Chapter 4

# "I'M GOING TO FLORIDA"

After the three of us had been initiated into the Entered Apprentice Degree we were immediately assigned an instructor from among the experienced brothers in the Lodge. He was to meet with us at least once weekly at the Lodge Hall for several weeks[1] to instruct and coach us in the necessary memory work until we were ready to recite before the Lodge and actually have the degree conferred.

This memory work consisted of portions of the initiation ritual (in which we had been prompted during initiation, or had simply had them shown us or spoken for us), such as the secret word, dueguard, sign, grip, and the oath (obligation). Then, when we were ready, we would be examined orally before the Lodge, the questions being put to us by our instructor.

Our final examination for the Entered Apprentice Degree would be given on the same night that we would be initiated into the Fellowcraft Degree, making for a very long meeting on that night.

The instructor set a regular night for the three of us to meet with him and I was looking forward to it. I was definitely motivated, an eager beaver, ready to "get on with it." I wanted to take the oral exam for Entered Apprentice and be initiated into the Fellowcraft Degree as soon as possible.

Meanwhile, Roy, a friend with whom I had been in the Army,

called me. He was living in South Florida in one side of a duplex house. The other side was empty. He urged Bonnie and me to leave the North, with its long, cold winters and come to Florida with him and his family. He painted a most appealing picture and said he was sure we could both find jobs there.

We really didn't want to leave, for the city was "home" to us. Both of us had grown up there and what families we had were there. So I just went ahead with my job at the post office and looked forward to the training sessions with our instructor at the Lodge Hall. I believed that I would soon be ready, with the other two men, to take the examination. I kept thinking about Roy and what he had suggested, but it was just too big a change to make so lightly.

## ONE COLD NIGHT

Christmas had come and gone, then New Year's Day, and the post office still kept me on. I was working second shift, from 3 to 11 P.M., on the south side of town where packages were handled. The weather was extremely cold.

One bitterly cold night, when my shift was over, I walked out to the parking lot to get into my car and drive home as I always did. When I tried to start the car it wouldn't do a thing; it was frozen. A lot of the gasoline being sold at the time had water in it and I was the victim of a tank full. The fuel line and the carburetor were frozen and it simply wouldn't start. I was stranded in the middle of a very cold winter night.

There was no one left in the lot to give me a ride, so there was nothing to do but walk to town where I could catch a streetcar home.

I locked the car, wrapped my coat around me and set out for town, walking into a cold north wind. As I walked along on painfully cold feet I began thinking of Roy and his proposal. The more I thought of it, the more attractive the thoughts of that warm climate became.

Soon, with each step I was saying to myself, "I'm going to Florida, I'm going to Florida, I'm going to Florida," keeping cadence with my steps crunching on the frozen ground. With each step I was more determined to do it and by the time I reached town, and the first streetcar stop, the decision was made. We were going to Florida, and the sooner the better!

When I presented the idea to Bonnie she was willing and immediately we began to make preparations. Thoughts of how this would affect my progress as a Mason didn't have much impact; that could be worked out somehow. The cold weather and contrasting thoughts of palm trees, warm breezes and orange groves prevailed. We were going to Florida at least until the awful winter was over.

Within a few weeks we were on our way south. We drove through Kentucky, Tennessee and Georgia. The farther south we drove the warmer it was and the happier I became. It felt so "right."

## A TEMPORARY STANDSTILL

In Florida we moved right into the other side of the duplex Roy and his family were in and settled down. I was in contact with the Lodge back home and they thought I would soon be back. So did I but I felt no compulsion to be in a hurry about it. My degree instructor finally wrote and told me that the other two men who had been initiated as Entered Apprentices with me were already Master Masons (had completed the first three degrees); he wanted to know when I would be coming back and was concerned that I would not be able to remember the material after so long a time. Actually, I did remember it — very well — for I frequently went over all of it in my mind. I remembered it though I had not been able to attend even the first training session with the instructor before leaving for Florida.

It was suggested that I might be able to go on with the degree work right there in Florida so I inquired about it. I learned that, with a letter from the Lodge back home, I could continue in Florida as a "courtesy candidate" and finish all three degrees right there. Since I had already paid for all three of the Blue Degrees,[2] it wouldn't cost me anything to take the degrees in Florida. I was delighted, made the necessary arrangements, and immediately commenced the memory work with an instructor from the local lodge.

## SO WHY LEAVE?

Meanwhile, I applied for a job with the City Port Authority and was accepted. Bonnie had a good job, already, and we were doing fine. Spring had come and cold weather was over back home but thoughts of returning to the North were rapidly losing their appeal. We talked it over, discussed it with Roy and his wife and considered the facts that we both had good jobs where we were, had no jobs back home, and liked Florida better each day. So, we reasoned, why leave? We decided to stay right where we were, at least for the foreseeable future.

## BACK INTO THE CRAFT

It may seem that my ardent seeking into Freemasonry had been interrupted, that it had been displaced in my life's goals and values, but it hadn't been — not at all. I had been preoccupied with the move to Florida and the search for a good job there, but actually all this had only involved a few months. I had continued to rehearse the secret degree work in my mind all the while and I had kept in touch with the Lodge in Indianapolis. There had been a little "time out," but no real change in my heart.

With my acceptance by the Florida Lodge as a courtesy candidate for the rest of the Blue Degrees, I stepped right back into my active pursuit of the Masonic mountaintop.

I was soon ready for the oral examination for the Entered Apprentice Degree and initiation into the Fellowcraft Degree. I had never ceased to remember and to prepare, and was anxious to proceed with it.

## A FELLOWCRAFT MASON

Although I was now in another Grand Lodge (each state is a separate "Grand Lodge" and, in many ways, independent of the others) and in the Southern Jurisdiction[3], things were essentially the same in Florida and I felt a basic familiarity with what was happening as I was being prepared for the Fellowcraft initiation. When I arrived at the Lodge Hall and was led into the Preparation Room I was much more relaxed than I had been that first time a few months earlier in Indianapolis. There were three other men to be examined with me, including one who had previously taken the examination and failed it. We waited in our street clothes while the Worshipful Master opened the Lodge in the Master Mason's

Degree (the Lodge is always opened in the Master Mason's degree when candidates are to be examined for the Blue Degrees). Then the Lodge was "called off" to the Entered Apprentice Degree for the examination and the Senior Deacon escorted us into the Lodge Hall, placing us near the altar.

Our instructor had now changed roles and become our examiner, as we had known he would do. He took his place at the west side of the altar, facing us, and began to ask us the questions for which we had been prepared. No one of us was asked all the questions; but, of course, it was necessary for each of us to know all the answers for we couldn't know which ones we would be asked.

We answered his questions in order, without a flaw, and were then escorted back to the Preparation Room to wait while the Lodge members voted on whether to award the degree to us.[4]

After a rather short time, the Junior Deacon came into the Preparation Room and told us that we had all been accepted and awarded the Entered Apprentice Degree. We were all pleased, but not too surprised, and were immediately told to remove our clothes to prepare for initiation into the Fellowcraft (Second) Degree. We undressed and were given pajama tops and bottoms, very similar to those I remembered from the Entered Apprentice initiation, and, again, one slipper. This time, however, we were told to put the one slipper on the left foot, leaving the right one bare. The right leg of the trousers was rolled up above the knee and the right arm left out of the top leaving the right side of the torso naked.

We were ready, but this time I was not to be first; the man who had failed and been forced to retake his examination was taken into the Lodge Room for initiation first.

When the first man had completed the initiation, put his street clothes back on and been seated in the Lodge Hall to watch the rest of us, it was my turn.

I was hoodwinked, just like before. But when the cabletow was tied onto me it was not put around my neck; instead, it was wound twice around my right arm. The Steward led me to the inner door and told me to give three raps. After a brief delay, there were three answering raps on the other side of the door. The Steward opened the door just enough to allow discussion and the question was asked (it was the Senior Deacon, as in the first degree), "Who comes here?"

The Steward, who was holding onto me, replied, "A brother who has been regularly initiated an Entered Apprentice and now desires to receive additional light in Masonry by being passed to the degree of Fellowcraft."

I was then asked by the Senior Deacon, "Is this an act of your own free will and accord?" and I replied, "It is."

This time things were not so strange and new; in fact, I could anticipate some of it before it took place. I was much more relaxed. The Senior Deacon asked the Steward if I were duly and truly prepared and if I were well qualified.

To both, the Steward replied that I was.

The Senior Deacon asked the Steward if I had made suitable proficiency in the preceding degree, and was told that I had. The Senior Deacon then asked "by what further right or benefit" I expected to gain admission. The Steward replied, "By benefit of the Pass."

The Steward was then asked if I had the pass and replied that I did not, but that he had it for me.

The door was opened just enough for the Steward to whisper the password to the Senior Deacon who then said, "Let him wait until the Worshipful Master is informed of his request and his answer returned."

The door was closed. After a short delay the door was opened and the Senior Deacon said from right in front of me that it was the will of the Worshipful Master that I enter the Lodge of Fellowcrafts and that I be received "in due and ancient form." That part sounded very familiar.

The Senior Deacon then said to me, "My brother, it is the will of the Worshipful Master that you be received into this Lodge upon the angle of a square at your naked right breast, which is to teach you that the square of virtue should be a rule and guide to your conduct in all your future action with mankind and more especially with a brother Mason. "

As he was saying this, he pressed the point of the square into my bare chest; it was uncomfortable, but nothing like as painful as the compass points pressed into me in the first initiation. He then took me firmly by my bare right arm and began to lead me around the room. It is awkward to walk in a strange place blindfolded, even when being led along; there is always the thought that you are about to run into something.

In this way I made my way around the Lodge Hall and, as we passed certain places, I heard tapping sounds, two each time. We seemed to be going around again, and this time stopped (at the station of the Junior Warden) and there were three taps. The same questions and answers that were exchanged at the door were repeated.

Then the Junior Warden asked, "Has he the password?"

The Senior Deacon replied, "He has it not; I have it for him."

Upon being told to advance and give the password, the Senior Deacon did so, saying "SHIBBOLETH." The Junior Warden replied, "Right. Pass on."

We began moving again and stopped as before (this time it was at the station of the Senior Warden). The same questions and answers were exchanged and the Senior Warden directed that I be conducted to the Worshipful Master in the East for final instruction. We began moving again and stopped at the Master's station. Here the very same questions were asked and the very same replies given. (The similarity with the Entered Apprentice initiation ritual was apparent to me, even at the time.) The Worshipful Master then directed that I be returned to the Senior Warden in the West who would instruct me in the proper manner in which to approach the East. So back to the Senior Warden's station we went and he said that the Senior Deacon should so instruct me.

The thought that this was a wasted trip flickered across my mind when the Senior Deacon turned me around (facing the East) and told me to step off with my left foot as an Entered Apprentice, then take a step with my right foot, bringing the heel of my left foot up to the hollow (instep) of the right one, forming the angle of an oblong square (the Tau Cross).

This was just the way I had done it in the first initiation, except that the extra step resulted in reversing the Tau Cross made with my feet. Then, as before, the Senior Deacon suddenly and loudly said in my ear, "STAND ERECT!" This time I rather expected it, so wasn't startled as I was the first time, but it still had a strange effect on me that I didn't understand.

Then the Worshipful Master began to speak from directly in front of me. He said that our knowledge as Masons is progressive and our obligation is similarly progressive and binding. But he gave me the same assurance as had been given in the Entered Apprentice initiation that nothing in my oath or obligation would conflict with my duty to my God, my country, my neighbor or myself, but said it would merely bind me more closely to the brothers of the Lodge.

He then asked me whether, with that assurance, I were willing to proceed, and I said, "I am." He then told the Senior Deacon to place me "in due form" at the altar to be made a Fellowcraft.

The Senior Deacon said to me, "Advance! Kneel on your naked right knee, your left forming a square, your body erect, your right hand resting on the Holy Bible, square and compass, your left elbow forming a right angle, supported by the square." He helped me to get into this position, and then said to the Master, "The candidate is in due form, Worshipful Master." There were three raps of a gavel, some shuffling noises, and the Master said, "You will repeat your name and repeat after me: "I, James D. Shaw, of my own free will and accord, in the presence of Almighty God and this Worshipful Lodge, do hereby and hereon solemnly and sincerely promise and swear." I reaffirmed the oath that I had taken as an Entered Apprentice and swore not to reveal any of the secrets of a Fellowcraft Mason to any Entered Apprentice or to any "profane person."[5] I promised to abide by the laws, rules and regulations of a Fellowcraft Lodge and that I would respond to degree. Then I swore not to cheat or defraud, knowingly, a Fellowcraft Lodge or a brother of that degree. [6] To all this I swore, "binding myself under no less a penalty than that of having my left breast torn open, my heart plucked out and given to the beasts of the field and fowls of the air as a prey" should I ever knowingly or willingly violate the oath.

The Worshipful Master then said, "In token of your sincerity, kiss the Holy Bible open before you." As I had done in the first initiation, I leaned forward and kissed the Bible. It gave me a strange sensation.

The Master then told the Senior Deacon that, since I was bound to the Lodge by an oath which cannot be broken (a bond much stronger than any rope) that he was to remove the cabletow from my arm. As soon as it was removed, the Master asked me what I most desired. Prompted by the Senior Deacon, I replied, "Further light" (by this time, I knew better than to ask for cold water).

The Master then said, "Further light being your desire, you shall receive it." As in the first degree, the brothers came down and lined up on either side of me and, as they and the Master clapped their hands, the hoodwink was removed from my eyes. Then the Master called my attention to the fact that this time one point of the compass was hidden beneath the square, which was to teach me that there were still more secrets hidden from my view. He then approached the altar and demonstrated the due-guard and sign of a Fellowcraft Mason. The due-guard consisted of the right arm extended, just below the chest, palm-down, and the left arm raised to form a right angle, just as mine had been while taking the oath. The sign was given by raising the right hand to the left breast and drawing it swiftly across the chest as if tearing it open with claws and then dropping the hand to the side, all in one motion.

The Master then extended his right hand to me "in token of brotherly love and confidence" and demonstrated the pass grip by shaking hands and pressing his thumb between the first and second fingers where they join the hand. He gave me the word, the name of the pass grip, "SHIBBOLETH."

Next came the "real grip," made by putting the thumb on the first knuckle of the second finger so that each can stick the nail of his thumb into the knuckle of the other. The name was given to me as "JACHIN," spoken in the following manner.

While giving the grip, you say, "What is this?"; the answer is "A grip." Then, "A grip of what?"; the reply is "The grip of a Fellowcraft Mason." Question: "Has it a name?"; reply: "It has." Next you say, "Give it me." Reply: "I will letter it or halve it." Then you say, "Halve it and begin." Answer: "Nay, you begin." Again you say, "You begin." The reply: "Ja." My response: "Chin." Then he replies: "Jachin; right brother, I greet you." It was all so complicated but I could only accept it.

Then the Master got an apron and put it on me with appropriate remarks about its importance. The Senior Warden tucked the lower left corner under the top. I was then excorted by the Senior Deacon to the station of the Worshipful Master in the East who presented and explained the significance of "the tools of a Fellowcraft Mason," the plumb, square, and level, applying them to principles of virtue and morality.

He then said, "I further present you with three precious jewels; their names are Faith, Hope and Charity. They teach us to have faith in the Grand Architect of the Universe, hope in immortality and charity to all mankind, more especially a brother Mason."

Then he directed the Senior Deacon to conduct me "out of the Lodge Room" and to "reinvest him with that of which he has been divested" (in ordinary language, to take me back to the Preparation Room and let me put my clothes back on).

My Fellowcraft initiation was almost completed, and I was feeling pretty good about it.

When I had re-dressed I was readmitted to the Lodge Hall and seated. I was told that our forefathers, the ancient Masonic brethren, worked at the building of King Solomon's Temple and many other edifices, Masonic buildings, cathedrals and the like.

The Senior Deacon described the two columns (or pillars) of the Temple, said the name of the left one is Boaz, and that of the right one Jachin. He also went into considerable detail in describing the symbolic significance of the decorations on them.

Then the Master said that I had been admitted to the "Middle Chamber" of King Solomon's Temple for the explanation of the letter "G." He said that it denotes "Deity" before whom we ought all to bow in reverence to worship and adore. He said that it also denotes "Geometry" by means of which "we may track Nature through her various windings to her most concealed recesses." He said that by means of geometry we may better comprehend the perfection of Nature and the "goodness of the Great Artificer of the Universe."

With this brief lecture on the letter "G" my initiation ended and I watched as the remaining candidate was initiated. As was the case when I was initiated into the Entered Apprentice Degree, my watching the other man not only helped me to understand it all better, but helped me to be off to a good start in memorizing it all for my coming examination in the degree. I was back on the Masonic pathway and picking up speed.

## Footnotes

[1]The exact amount of time required for this varies depending on how quickly the candidate can memorize the material required, but is usually completed in 4-6 weeks.

[2]Basic Freemasonry consists of the first three degrees: Entered Apprentice, Fellowcraft, and Master Mason. These constitute the foundation of all Masonry and are conferred and conducted in the local, hometown lodge. The lodge is referred to as "Blue Lodge," and the first three degrees as the "Blue Degrees," because of the importance of the blue sky and its heavenly host of stars and planets. Astrology is extremely important to Masonry, and it is also important that ancient pagans worshiped on high places (hill tops) "under the starry canopy of heaven."

[3]American Freemasonry (Blue Lodge and Scottish Rite) is divided into two jurisdictions. The Northern Jurisdiction includes 15 northern and northeastern states; the much-larger Southern Jurisdiction includes the other 35 states, plus all U.S. territories and trusts.

[4]This voting is done with white and black balls, dropped into a box. A white ball is a "yes" vote, and a black ball is a "no" vote. If there is even one black ball in the box, the candidate is not accepted for the degree. All such voting is done while the Lodge is in session in the Master Mason (3rd) degree, and only 3rd Degree (Master) Masons can take part.

[5]All non-Masons are, according to Masonic law and tradition, "profane" persons. This includes the Mason's wife, children and parents, unless they, too, are Masons. The English word "profane" is derived from the Latin word "profanis," meaning "before, or outside, the temple," hence not holy, not clean, debased and unworthy, a thing to be avoided for it would contaminate the holy and clean ones. If you are not a Mason, this is what you are to the Masonic world. See, in this regard, I Timothy 1:9-11 for the Bible meaning of "profane."

[6]Note that there is no promise not to cheat or defraud the "profane." That seems to be accepted in Masonic morality. See Appendix C, "Masonic Morality."

# Chapter 5

# MASTER MASON

For the next two weeks the three of us attended training sessions at the Lodge three nights a week. Once again, it seemed easy and natural for me to learn the secret degree work. I was glad to have the first two degrees behind me and was eager to get on with the work and become a Master Mason. I really liked the growing sense of acceptance my commitment to the Lodge gave me; those men were devoting time and energy to me and my progress in the Craft and the feeling of belonging did something good for me — something I had wanted for a very long time and not known.

At the end of two weeks (which passed very quickly) we met at the Lodge for our examination in the Fellowcraft Degree and initiation into the Master Mason Degree. Once again, we waited in the Preparation Room in our street clothes while the Worshipful Master opened the lodge in the Master Mason's Degree and then "called it off" to the Fellowcraft Degree for examination.

The Senior Deacon escorted us into the Lodge Hall and placed us, as before, facing the altar and the Worshipful Master. Our instructor, who was now our examiner, stood (as before) facing us with his back to the altar. I felt a strange mixture of apprehension and eager confidence — like a well-trained athlete at the start of a race. I was ready.

The examiner questioned us in turn and we all gave the correct answers; although no one of us was asked all of the questions, I

**43**

could have answered them all. We were then escorted back into the Preparation Room to await the voting by the membership.

They didn't take much time in the voting and the Junior Deacon came into the room to announce that we had all been accepted. There had been no black balls in the ballot box; "the ballot was clear." We were Fellowcraft Masons!

Immediately I was told to remove my clothes and prepare for initiation into the Master Mason degree. The others would be initiated in the following weeks; I was to be initiated alone. I put on the same pajama-like bottoms as before, but this time both legs were rolled up above the knees: and both feet were left bare. I was not given the shirt to put on and was left naked above the waist. The cabletow was wound about my body three times at the waist and then I was hoodwinked. I could see nothing at all — not even any light.

The same questions as before were asked and answered at the door and I was led through the door and into the Lodge Room. The Senior Deacon said, "Brother James, you are received into this Lodge of Master Masons upon the points of the compass extending from your right to left breast, which is to teach you that, as the most vital parts of the man are contained between the breasts, so are the most valuable tenets of Masonry contained between the two extreme points of the compass, which are virtue, morality and brotherly love." The compass points were sharp and I felt them as he made his teaching points.

After being received at the door, I was led to the Worshipful Master who asked for the password. The Senior Deacon, in a whisper, communicated it to him, for me, "Tubal-Cain." Then I was led by the Senior Deacon around the room as before, stopping at the station of the Junior Warden, who sent me to the Senior Warden, who then directed that I be placed at the altar in due form to receive the obligation. I was led to the altar and stood waiting.

From directly in front of me the Master spoke, giving again the assurance that there was nothing in the oath that would conflict with my other duties and commitments; and, once again, I had no way of knowing that what he was saying could not possibly be true.

Asked, as before, if I were willing to proceed with the oath, I replied "I am," and he directed the Senior Deacon to place me "in due form" at the altar to be made a Master Mason.

## TAKING THE MASTER MASON OATH

The Senior Deacon placed me in position, kneeling this time on both bare knees, body erect, legs forming a square, both hands resting on the square and compass upon the Bible.

Told that I was "in due form" to receive the obligation, the Worshipful Master had me repeat after him, a few words at a time, the oath of obligation: "I, James D. Shaw, of my own free will and accord in the Presence of Almighty God and this Worshipful Lodge, do hereby and hereon solemnly promise and swear; that I will always hail, ever conceal and never reveal, any of the secret arts, parts or points of the Master Mason's degree to any person or persons whomsoever except it be to a true and lawful brother of this degree and not unto him or them until after due trial and strict examination I have found him or them justly entitled to receive the same. I furthermore promise and swear that I will conform and abide by all the laws, rules and regulations of the Master Mason's degree, and of the Lodge of which I shall hereafter become a member, and that I will ever maintain and support the constitution, laws and edicts of the Grand Lodge under whom the same shall work, so far as they shall come to my knowledge. Furthermore, that I will keep the secrets of a worthy Master Mason as inviolable as my own, when communicated to and received by me as such. Furthermore, I will aid and assist all worthy distressed brother Master Masons, their widows and orphans, I knowing them to be such, so far as their necessities may require and my ability will permit without material injury to myself. Furthermore, that I will not assist in, nor be present at, the initiating, passing or raising of a woman, an old man in his dotage, a young man in his non-age, a madman or a fool, I knowing them to be such. I furthermore promise and swear I will not visit a clandestine lodge of Freemasons, nor converse Masonically with a clandestine Mason, or with one who has been expelled or suspended, while under that sentence, knowing them to be such.

"I furthermore promise and swear that I will not cheat, wrong or defraud a lodge of Master Masons or a brother of this degree, knowing them to be such, but will give them due and timely notice that they may ward off all approaching danger. I furthermore promise and swear that I will not violate the chastity of a Master Mason's wife, his mother, sister, or daughter, knowing them to be such.[1] I furthermore promise and swear that I will not give the Grand Masonic Word in any other manner than that in which I shall receive it, which shall be on the five points of fellowship and at low breath. I furthermore promise and swear that I will not give the Grand Hailing Sign of Distress except it be in case of most imminent danger, my life in peril, or within a lawfully constituted lodge of Masons. When I hear the words spoken and see the sign given, I will hasten to the aid of the one giving it if there be a greater possibility of saving his life than that of losing my own.

"To all of the which, I do most sincerely promise and swear with a firm and steadfast resolution to keep and perform the same, without the least equivocation, mental reservation or self-evasion whatever, binding myself under no less a penalty than that of having my body severed in twain, my bowels taken out and burned to ashes, the ashes scattered to the four winds of heaven that there should be no more remembrance among men and Masons forever of so vile a wretch as I should be, should I ever knowingly or wittingly violate or transgress this my solemn and binding Master Mason's obligation. So help me God and keep me steadfast."

As had been the case with the oaths of obligation of the first two degrees, I had no idea of what I would be swearing to do until I was actually hearing and repeating each line. Had I been able to hear or read the oath in advance, I might not have been able to say it. Even while taking it as I did, one might expect that the nature of parts of it would have made me hesitate; but I really wasn't thinking of the nature of the oath. I was thinking of Uncle Irvin and how I was now going to be a good and successful man as I supposed him to be. If mother were alive, she would be pleased.

## BUT THERE WAS MORE

Upon completion of the oath, the Master came down to the altar. He directed the Senior Deacon to remove the cabletow from around my waist since I was now bound by my obligation to the Lodge. He then asked me what I most desired; prompted, I replied "More light." He replied that, since that was my desire, that was what I should receive. As the hoodwink was suddenly removed, the brothers (assembled as before) clapped their hands in unison and my eyes were again dazzled by the sudden bright light. Even though this had happened to me twice before, it was still somewhat startling and disorienting. It was as if a susceptibility or fear had been planted in me the first time and it remained.

The Master then instructed me in making the sign which was made by dropping the left hand to my side, bringing the right hand to the left of my waist, palm- down, and then bringing it quickly across my waist as if severing my body in twain with my thumb, then dropping my right hand to the side.

I was shown to make the due-guard by extending the hands, palm-down, as they had been placed on the square and compasss while taking the oath. The pass grip was shown me by grasping the hand in the normal (handshake) way, but pressing the thumb between the second and third joints of the fingers where they join the other's hand. The name of the pass was then given me: "Tubal-Cain."

Thinking I was just about finished with the Master Mason initiation, feeling I was "down to the short rows," I was both listening to the Worshipful Master and feeling a growing sense of pleasant release. I had it made, I thought, and it had been so easy!

I was given an apron and the Senior Warden helped me to put it on as a Master Mason with the "bib" hanging down in front. I was then returned to the preparation room and told to take off the initiation drawers I was in and put my street clothes back on, with the apron.

A plumb emblem, the Junior Warden's "Jewel," was put around my neck; I was now dressed as a Master Mason. I looked myself over as best I could, and was thinking, "Wow! I am a Master Mason at last!"

It was a heady moment and I was exhilarated. But my newfound sense of having arrived didn't last long. I was told that I must be returned to the Lodge Room for further instruction.

## AN UNEXPECTED DISAPPOINTMENT

Back inside the Lodge Room, still feeling very pleased and proud to be a Master Mason, feeling the exciting newness of wearing the Master Mason's apron and with the plumb emblem around my neck, I was taken to a position before the Worshipful Master.

He said to me, "You have been taught to wear your apron as a Master Mason and you are doing so at the moment. This would imply you are a Master Mason and qualified to travel and work as such. Nay, more, I observe that you have upon your person the badge of office, the Jewel of the Junior Warden, one of the principal officers of the Lodge. This mark of distinction must be highly pleasing to you and doubtless you now consider yourself a Master Mason. Is that not so?"

Suddenly the exhilaration left me and fear took its place. Something was going on that I hadn't expected. I was afraid to say "yes," so I said nothing at all. The Senior Deacon then answered for me, saying, "He is of that opinion, Worshipful Master." The Master then said to me, "It is my duty to tell you that you are *not yet* a Master Mason, nor do I know that you will *ever* be. The road you must travel in order to prove yourself is a long, hard and rough one, upon which lives have been lost, and you may lose yours."

Well, that ended any doubts I had about whether my initiation was over; now I *knew* I was not yet finished. I was not yet a Master Mason and what he said about losing my life sounded ominous. With that strange fear still stirring within me, I was led to the altar and told to kneel and pray for myself, either silently or out loud. I had no idea how to pray, so I just knelt silently with my head bowed and waited.

## LIVING OUT THE LEGEND

After kneeling and waiting silently, appearing to pray, I was told to remove all articles from my pockets, take off my watch, and to lay them all on the altar. The hoodwink was once again put over my eyes and I couldn't see a thing.

The Senior Deacon then said to me, "My brother, heretofore you have represented a candidate in search of MORE LIGHT; now you will represent another character, no less a personage than our Grand Master Hiram Abiff[2], Grand Master and architect at the building of King Solomon's Temple. It was the custom of this great and good man, at high twelve, when the craft were called from labor to refreshment, to enter the Holy of Holies, to offer up his adorations to Deity and draw his designs upon his trestle board."

All the time he was telling me this, he was leading me around the room. Trying to listen and understand while stumbling along blindfolded was difficult and awkward for me.

He continued, "He then passed out by way of the South Gate to talk to the workmen, as you will do now."

After being led a few more steps, I was accosted by a brother representing the character Jubela, (it was actually the Junior Warden). He spoke to me as if I were actually Hiram Abiff, and grabbed me by the lapels. He said that I had promised to reveal the secret word of a Master Mason when the Temple was completed, that it was nearly completed, and demanded that I give him the secret word then and there. All the while, as he spoke roughly to me, he was jerking me around and really roughing me up.

The Senior Deacon, speaking for me, said, "Craftsman, this is neither the time nor the place. Wait until the Temple is finished and then you shall have the secrets of a Master Mason."

Jubela then got even more violent, demanding the secret word, right then! Again speaking for me, the Senior Deacon said, "Craftsman, I cannot and will not give them," upon which Jubela struck a blow across my throat with the 24-inch gauge. It hurt and startled me and I was immediately hurried a few steps farther where I was stopped and grabbed by a second "ruffian," called Jubelo. This one *really* jerked me around, and said, "Grand Master Hiram Abiff, the craft are waiting and many are exceedingly anxious to receive the secrets of a Master Mason, and we see no good reason why we are put off so long. We have determined that we will wait no longer. I therefore *demand* of you the secrets of a Master Mason!"

Again speaking for me, the Senior Deacon said, "Craftsman, why all this violence? When the Temple is finished, you shall receive this secret word; I cannot, nor will not, give them to you at this time."

Jubelo then became even more furious and again demanded the word, upon which the Senior Deacon answered for me, "I cannot give them nor can they be given except in the presence of three: Solomon, King of Israel; Hiram, King of Tyre; and myself."

Jubelo, becoming *still more* violent, reminded me that there was no one there to help me and threatened to kill me if I didn't give him the word.

For me, the Senior Deacon replied, "My life you may take, but my integrity, *never!*"

Jubelo then struck a heavy blow across my chest with the square. It hurt, but I was immediately jerked away and led a few more steps when I was grabbed a third time and shaken. This was all very real, even though it was obvious that parts were being acted out. I was being jerked about, shoved, shouted at and hit by people I couldn't see. I had great difficulty in keeping my balance (if the "ruffians" hadn't been holding onto my coat I would have fallen many times), and the violence was even more shocking because I couldn't see it coming.

The third "ruffian," Jubelum, said as he was shaking me that he had heard me speaking to Jubela and Jubelo and saw that I had escaped, but said I would *not* escape from him *ever*. He said that what he said, he would do, and that he held in his hand "an instrument of death." He said that if I didn't give him the secrets of a Master Mason immediately he would kill me.

Speaking for me again, the Senior Deacon replied as he had already replied to Jubela and Jubelo. Jubelum then shouted at me, "For the last time, Grand Master Hiram, give me the secret word or I will take your life!"

I, of course, didn't realize it, but as Jubelum readied himself to deliver the death blow, several of the brothers moved into position behind me, holding a large canvas, stretched out so as to catch me when I fell.

With that, Jubelum shouted, "If you will not give me the secret word of a Master Mason, then...DIE!"

As he shouted the word, "DIE," he hit me right in the middle of my forehead with a setting maul! I saw stars. They were brilliant and in colors, and I fell backward onto the canvas, unconscious. [3]

I wasn't out very long and I came to, head still ringing and aching, with the three "ruffians" standing around me, talking over the situation, and discussing how to dispose of the body. They decided to conceal the body "in the rubbish of the Temple" until "low twelve" (midnight), when they would meet and decide what to do. So they carried me, on the canvas, a little distance and covered me with "rubbish," consisting of chairs and other objects in the Lodge Hall. There was silence, then I heard a bell strike 12 times and the "ruffians" returned. Jubela said, "This is the hour."

Jubelo said, "This is the place." Jubelum then said, "And there is the body. Assist me to carry it in a due west course from the temple to the brow of a hill where I have dug a grave, six feet due east and west, and six feet perpendicular, in which we shall bury it."

They removed the chairs and other "Temple rubbish" from me, picked me up on the canvas, carried me to the west side of the Lodge Room and laid me down between the stations of the Master and the Senior Warden, my feet to the east. They lowered me to the floor a little at a time, pausing three times, to simulate lowering me into a grave.

After I was "buried," Jubelum said, "I will set this sprig of Acacia at the head of the grave, that the place may be known should the occasion require it. And now let us make our escape out of the country by the way of Joppa. We should be able to get a ship to take us to a foreign port."

The "ruffians" then acted out a scene in which they talked with a sea captain and asked for passage on his ship which was to sail the next day. Learning they could not sail without a pass from King Solomon, they decided to flee into the mountains and hide.

Meanwhile, the Worshipful Master, acting the part of King Solomon, heard a lot of commotion made by other brothers acting as workmen in the Temple. Solomon asked what the noise was all about and was told that Grand Master Hiram Abiff was missing and could not be found.

King Solomon ordered that a search be made and the brothers then did a lot of talking back and forth while I lay there, saying such things as, "Have you seen him?" "Not since high twelve yesterday," and, "Where is our Grand Master?"

Then King Solomon ordered that a search be made with one party going west, one east, one north, and one south. At this point there were three loud raps on the door and when the "alarm was attended" there were found to be 12 "fellowcrafts" who confessed to the King that they and three others had conspired to force Hiram to reveal the secret word. They said that they (the 12) had not been able to go through with their evil plan, having "reflected with horror on the atrocity of the crime," but reported that the other three had gone through with it.

The King then sent out those 12, three in each direction, to search for Jubela, Jubelo and Jubelum. One group of three spoke with the sea captain and, following the direction he gave them, followed the murderers' path and found the new grave, marked with the Acacia sprig. Digging down, they "discovered" my body.

Reporting to Solomon, they were sent back to identify the body and, if Hiram, to raise it with the grip of an Entered Apprentice.

As the drama continued, they returned to the "grave" and saw that I was indeed Hiram[4]; but they could not "raise" me, as the body was decomposing, so the "flesh left the bone." They reported the problem to Solomon, who sent them back to raise the body with the grip of a Fellowcraft. When "the skin (slipped) away" they reported this failure to Solomon.

Then the Master, playing King Solomon, came over to me and took my hand with the grip of a Master Mason, "the strong grip of the lion's paw"[5] and, with the other hand behind my back, assisted me to a standing position. I was fully recovered by this time, but still stiff and a little wobbly from the strain and from lying still for so long while the latter part of the drama was acted out.

The Master explained that while the secret word of the Master Mason had been lost when Hiram was killed, the first word he spoke when raised from the dead was the substitute for the "lost word." He then placed his right foot alongside mine, instep to instep, his knee against mine, his chest against mine and his mouth next to my right ear. With my hand placed on his back, we were "on the five points of fellowship: foot to foot, knee to knee, chest to chest, hand to back and mouth to ear." He whispered into my ear the Grand Masonic Word, "Mah-Hah-Bone," and instructed me that it must never be given to any but another Master Mason, only "on the five points of fellowship" as he had given it to me and never above a whisper, under penalty of death.

I was then instructed by the Worshipful Master in giving the "Grand Hailing Sign of Distress." The Grand Hailing Sign of Distress is given by raising the hands above the head and looking up, then lowering the hands in supplication, then dropping them to the side. The words accompanying the sign are, "Oh, Lord my God, is there no help for the widow's son?"

He explained to me that I was never to give this sign unless in the most extreme distress and that it is the most important Masonic secret. I was reminded of the part of my obligation relating to my responsibility should another Master Mason ever give this sign to me and, with this, my initiation as a Master Mason was really finished at last.

With the instruction finished I was seated and there followed a rather long and involved lecture on the meaning of the symbols of a Master Mason and the lengthy charge of a Master Mason. When the Master closed the Lodge, the brothers crowded around me with congratulations and then went home.

Bonnie was waiting up for me and we shared the sense of accomplishment together. She was pleased and proud of me. It was a really wonderful moment of fulfillment. If only mother could know; I had a good job, a wonderful wife, and I had finally caught up with Uncle Irvin. I was a Master Mason.

### Footnotes

[1] *It is noteworthy when considering Masonic morality that the Master Mason swears that he will not have sexual intercourse with the wife, mother, daughter, or sister of another Master Mason, "knowing her to be such"; apparently this is alright with anyone else's wife, mother, daughter, or sister and is even all right with those of a Master Mason if unaware of the Masonic relationship. See Appendix C, "Masonic Morality."*

[2] *For the purpose and significance of this dramatization of the legend of Hiram Abiff, see Appendix D, "The Legend of Hiram Abiff."*

[3] *The man portraying Jubelum isn't supposed to hit the candidate that hard, but I was really knocked unconscious. The man who hit me was an undertaker, and we had many laughs later about his trying to drum up business in the Lodge while acting the part of Jubelum.*

[4] *In the drama, the Junior Warden's jewel (which was still around my neck) plays*

*a significant role in the candidate's being recognized as Hiram by the searchers.*

[5]*The Master's Grip, or the "Strong Grip of the Lion's Paw," was not explained to me; but I had felt it and, in watching subsequent initiations, I learned it. I later had occasions to use it as a Master Mason's pass grip, an alternate means of recognition to the primary grip explained by the Master that night. This grip is given by grasping the other's hand in the normal way, except that the thumb and small finger are wrapped around the edges of the hand, just below the thumb, with the middle three fingertips dug into the inside of the other's wrist. As Worshipful Master myself, later on, I, of course, used it in "raising the candidate."*

# Chapter 6

# GOING HIGHER

Before I was even through with the Master Mason degree, I had noticed and decided something: two things that would influence the rest of my life. I noticed that a great many Masons were not only content to stop at the Third Degree, but often came to Lodge and, after about 45 minutes, went to sleep and slept through the meetings. This offended me. What I decided was that I did not want to be that kind of Mason — *not ever!*

I was determined to learn and to grow, to keep moving on up in the fraternity, to climb the "Masonic mountain." At that early point in my Masonic career I really didn't know what there was to be accomplished. I didn't know what higher ground there was to be reached; but I knew that I didn't want to come to Lodge and sleep like those men did. Whatever there was to achieve, I wanted it. I was going higher!

## FROM CANDIDATE TO INSTRUCTOR

Within a month after I was raised to the Third Degree there was a new class of candidates to be brought through the Blue Degrees. I was still a "courtesy candidate" (Bonnie and I were still expecting to go back to Indianapolis before long), and grateful to that Lodge for bringing me through the Second and Third Degrees.

I was never bashful about such things, so I said to the Worshipful Master, "Sir, I am grateful to this Lodge and to you, and feel that I owe you something for what you have done for me. If you will appoint me, I will be glad to be the Instructor for this new class of candidates."

He thought a moment, looking at me intently, and then said that I had the job. I could hardly believe it. I had just been raised, a member of the most recent class, and now I was the Instructor! I thanked the Master and promised to do my very best. I could hardly wait to get started.

The next week we took the class through the Entered Apprentice initiation and they took their first obligation. The following week I arranged to meet with them for instruction and a month later they were ready to take their examination. They all passed, were then "passed" into the Fellowcraft Degree, and the week after that I began to instruct them in the memory work of that degree. At the end of that month they were ready for examination in the Fellowcraft Degree and again they all passed easily.

They were motivated and I had taught them well. Then, one each week, they were raised to the Master Mason degree and I had the satisfaction of knowing that I had brought the entire class through all three Blue Degrees. I was not only a Master Mason now, I was a *maker* of Master Masons. It really felt good.

## WHY LEAVE AT ALL?

By this time I had gone to work for the city and had an excellent job. Bonnie was well established in her job and was enjoying it. I was accepted in the Lodge and had a real sense of belonging. The more we thought and talked about it, the less reason we saw in leaving to go back to Indianapolis. There had been no hurry about leaving Florida and what we had found there through the winter and spring; and now, as we considered the situation, we asked ourselves, "Why shouldn't we just stay here? Why leave at all?"

So we decided: we would just settle in and stay right there. Florida would be our home. I would no longer be just a "courtesy candidate" or a visitor in the Lodge; it would be *my* Lodge. I would really *belong* there. With the decision made, we began to settle in and "get permanent."

Roy and his family moved to the west coast of Florida and we missed them, but that didn't matter so much now. We were making new friends in the Lodge.

## MOVING UP THROUGH THE CHAIRS

Not long after, elections were held in our Lodge and a new Worshipful Master was elected. I had already found out that there was a normal progression through the offices in the Lodge, beginning with the lowest office (Junior Steward) and proceeding up to the top (Worshipful Master). Since each office has a position (or "chair") in the Lodge Hall, this progression upward through the offices in the Blue Lodge is often called "moving up through the chairs." The positions of Junior and Senior Steward and Junior and Senior Deacon are appointed positions and men are selected for them by the Worshipful Master. The three top offices, Junior and Senior Warden and Worshipful Master, are elected positions. But the normal situation is that, once elected Junior Warden, that man will "move up." He can expect to move up to Senior Warden the following year and to the chair of Worshipful Master the year after that. Barring something unusual, these elections are virtually automatic.

As soon as I had the opportunity, I went to see the newly elected Worshipful Master and told him that I didn't want to be an "ordinary Mason." I said that I never wanted to be like those brothers who slept through the meetings and asked him to consider appointing me to a chair (an office) in the Lodge. I must have made a positive impression on him for he appointed me Senior Deacon, the highest appointed office in the Lodge. I had bypassed the three lowest offices and was off to a *big* head start in moving up through the chairs.

## BEYOND THE BLUE LODGE

Blue Lodge Masonry is the heart of Masonry and the Third Degree is the heart of the Blue Lodge. If one is not a Master Mason in good standing in the Blue Lodge, he cannot "go on" into the York Rite or the Scottish Rite and thence to "the top of the Masonic mountain." And, once advanced in the York Rite or the Scottish Rite, he cannot remain in those bodies (or the Shrine) if he doesn't continue in good standing in the Blue Lodge. This is the general structure and the Blue Lodge is its foundation.

I had been in the Blue Lodge about four months, had taken a class of candidates through all three degrees, and was Senior Deacon, learning, growing and feeling good about it when one day I was talking with a brother who owned a lumber yard.

He said, "I thought you joined the Masonic Lodge."

I said that I had and that I was very active.

He said something about the Scottish Rite and wondered why he hadn't seen me there.

I didn't know what he was talking about, but sensed that it was something I would want to do.

He said, "Jim, you've just got to get into the Scottish Rite, because you really don't know what Masonry is all about until you do. The Scottish Rite and its 29 degrees will really open your eyes." He said that if I wanted him to, he would get me a petition and get things rolling.

I said that it sounded good to me and asked him to go ahead. Although I was eager to begin, I found out that I couldn't enter the Scottish Rite until I had been a Master Mason for six months. But he went ahead with the petition while I waited. I went right on with my work in the Blue Lodge, the most eager and zealous man they had.

## 2 PATHS FROM WHICH TO CHOOSE

As I have already said, the Blue Lodge, with its three degrees, is the heart and foundation of Freemasonry. This is where the vast majority of Masons stop and go no farther, their local lodge being all they ever know of Masonry. However, for those who are not willing to stay at that level, there are two options for "going on higher," two paths to follow: they are the Scottish Rite and the York Rite.

The Scottish Rite includes 29 degrees beyond the Blue Lodge, culminating in the 32nd. The York Rite has the equivalent of the 29 degrees of the Scottish Rite and advancement along this path culminates in the degree "Knight Templar." In addition, the Shrine ("Ancient Arabic Order, Nobles of the Mystic Shrine") is available to 32nd Degree Masons and Knights Templar who wish to participate.

Devoted to community service and fun, the Shriners are looked upon as the "party boys" of Freemasonry and are best known for their hospitals for crippled children, for light-hearted participation in parades, and for their riotous, drunken parties and conventions.

Although at the time I was not fully aware of these options and how it all goes together, my path was determined. I was going into the Scottish Rite.

## INTO THE SCOTTISH RITE

The more my friend talked to me about the Scottish Rite, the more eager I was to get started in it. In the Scottish Rite, initiations are conducted and degrees conferred during meetings called "Reunions" which are normally held twice a year, fall and spring.

In addition to the initiations into the degrees, there is also recognition of those brothers who have died since the previous Reunion. They are, in this sense, memorials to the departed brothers. I could hardly wait for the Fall Reunion to come. As the time approached, I was told to report to the Secretary of the Scottish Rite for a briefing. I was there early, waiting for my turn to be called into his office.

The Secretary greeted me and explained the nature and structure of the Scottish Rite. He explained that the 29 degrees are divided into four groups called the "Four Bodies" of the Rite and that each of these bodies is somewhat like a separate lodge within the system. He also explained to me that the Reunion would last for four Sundays and that it would be possible for me to take all 29 degrees in the one Reunion, or just go to the 14th Degree at this Reunion and then continue to the 32nd Degree in the spring. He said that some men could not afford to take all of the degrees at one Reunion because of the cost. [1] He told me that the first of the four "bodies" of the Scottish Rite is called "Lodge of Perfection" and is the one in which business meetings are held on meeting nights. The second body, he said, is the "Chapter of Rose Croix," the third is the "Council of Kodosh" and the fourth is "The Consistory."

It all sounded wonderful to me and I asked the Secretary if I could just pay for all 29 of the degrees right then! He gave me the figure,

I wrote the check, and he told me to report on the next Sunday (the first day of the Fall Reunion). He told me that we would meet from 9 a.m. to 6 p.m. each Sunday for the next four Sundays to receive instruction, and that on the fourth Sunday I would be made a 32nd Degree Mason.

I asked him if I would have to memorize all the passwords, signs and grips and then pass examinations as we had to do in the Blue Lodge, and he *roared* with laughter!

He said, "Are you kidding? It would take you a whole *year* of Sundays to do that! You just be here Sunday and you will find out."

On the morning of the first Sunday of the Fall Reunion I arrived promptly and, as soon as all the rest arrived, we were ushered into a large classroom. There were about 250 of us and our class was given the name "George Washington Bicentennial Class" (each class is given a name, or title, which it retains as long as there are any of its members left alive).

Our instructor was an attorney, a man in his sixties. His age and knowledge made him seem a little "larger than life" to me, very impressive, and I listened carefully to all that he said. He also had a sense of humor, which made him even more effective. I was totally receptive.

We had to have an "opening ceremony" which gave our class official identity and status and then we had a class picture taken. We also had to elect class officers, but I didn't try for any of those offices as I was only interested in the degree work (the lessons in religion and morality). I wanted to *learn*.

## THROUGH THE DEGREES

With all the preliminaries completed, we were taken into the auditorium. It was like a large and very nice theater, with fully equipped stage, sophisticated lighting and theater seats. We were told to be seated and the presentation of the Fourth Degree began.

The Fourth Degree was put on just like a play, with one candidate chosen from the class to represent us all as he participated. The presentation went on until time to take the oath at the end. At this time we were told to stand, put our hands over our hearts and repeat the oath [2] of obligation with the representative candidate on the stage. After we finished the oath we were given the sign of that degree, [3] and the Fourth Degree was completed. When a degree is given in this way it is said to be "exemplified."

When a degree is not put on as a drama, but merely explained, it is said to be "communicated." Such was the case with the Fifth Degree. Back in the classroom the Degree Master explained the content and meaning of the degree, administered the oath, and gave us the sign.

Now we were Fifth Degree Masons, and ready for the Sixth Degree. And so we progressed, through the degrees. The relatively unimportant degrees, about one third of the total of 29, were "communicated" in this way. It is also true that some degrees which are merely "communicated" in one Reunion will be "exemplified" at the following Reunion. The degrees of the Four Bodies (the four degrees whose names identify the Four Bodies), however, are always put on in full and not merely "communicated." That Sunday we completed the Fourth through the Ninth Degrees and I went home feeling good about it all.

I was so interested in the degree work that I could hardly wait from one Sunday until the next. The "old religions" (the mystery religions of Egypt, Greece, Persia, etc.) were taught. And, as I had never had a religion, but had only heard passing references to the major ones, I was fascinated.

There was also a great deal said about the ancient philosophers and occultists and I felt that I was really growing in knowledge. Each week I would tell my brother Masons in the Blue Lodge how great it was and how much they were missing by not being in the Scottish Rite. But this was not always well-received; some were really offended and a few hurt, because they could not afford to go into the Rite. So, although my zeal didn't diminish any, I tried to be more careful about such enthusiastic talk.

On the second Sunday we completed the 14th degree, the Degree of Perfect Elu, generally considered the halfway mark in the Scottish Rite. With this attainment comes the 14th Degree ring. This flat gold band with the Hebrew letter "YOD" on it is the official Masonic ring.

Many kinds of rings with Masonic symbols may be purchased and worn; but, except for the Thirty-Third Degree ring, this ring is the only official one. It is the patent and property of the Supreme Council of the Thirty-Third Degree, and is only obtained when presented with the 14th degree. In our case the rings had not arrived so we had to wait to get them the final Sunday.

## ANOINTED A PRIEST AND A PROPHET

Finally, the last Sunday of Reunion arrived and we progressed to the 32nd Degree. Upon completion of the degree work, climaxing with the 32nd Degree lecture, we stood and were brought forward. One by one, we were anointed with oil. As the man placed his hand on my head and applied the oil, he said to me, "I anoint thee a Priest and a Prophet, and a Sublime Prince of the Royal Secret."

This part was definitely a new experience for me and I certainly didn't understand the part about being a priest and a prophet, but it was impressive and I liked the sound and solemnity of it. For me, it was rather awesome and a little unreal.

Each of us was presented, along with the Scottish Rite ring, a copy of Albert Pike's book, "Morals and Dogma." [4] We were told that it was *the* source book for Freemasonry and its meaning. We were also told that it must never leave our possession, and that arrangements must be made so that upon our deaths it would be returned to the Scottish Rite. It was clear that this book was not only a terribly important source but was, it seemed, almost sacred.

It had all been so very interesting to me and, in a way, the time had passed much too quickly. I felt that I had learned so much, yet felt that I had so much more to learn.

"Perhaps in the future I will get to *work* in these degrees," I thought."Then I can *really* learn about religions."

It was only about 5 p.m. when we finished and, after a lot of exchanging congratulations, I hurried home to tell Bonnie all about it (at least the parts I was free to tell her). As I headed home I was thinking, "If only mother had lived to see this day — she would really be proud."

## Footnotes

[1]There is a price to be paid, in dollars, for all "earned" Masonic degrees, from Entered Apprentice to the 32nd Degree. Dollar values change with time and fees vary some from place to place, but the total cost of going all the way to the 32nd Degree can be very substantial, well into the thousands of dollars today.

[2]There was a blood-oath of obligation for each degree, as in the Blue Lodge. Unlike the Blue Lodge, however, since there was no memorizing, and since they were not written down, the candidates normally remember nothing of these oaths once they are spoken.

[3]In all my years of Masonry that followed, I was never once asked to give this sign.

[4]Albert Pike (1809–1891) is easily the preeminent figure in American Freemasonry. His many titles included Sovereign Grand Commander of the Supreme Council of the Thirty-Third Degree (Mother Council of the World) and Supreme Pontiff of Universal Freemasony. Scholar, student of ancient languages and occult philosopher, he completely rewrote the degrees of the Scottish Rite into their present form. This work is explained in his book Morals and Dogma of the Ancient and Accepted Scottish Rite of Freemasonry. His position in Masonry was, and is today, unparalleled, not only in the United States, but throughout the world.

# Chapter 7

# BRANCHING OUT

The Monday after my initiation into the 32nd Degree, I was congratulated by a number of my superiors at work whom I had not even realized had been there. The extent of Masonry and its influence was far greater than I had suspected. Realizing that there were so many men such as these, seemingly everywhere, who were part of the Masonic brotherhood, and that they knew who I was and what I was doing, was both comforting and vaguely disturbing. But it was mostly comforting. I was seeing that this Masonic family of which I had become a committed part reached much farther into every part of life than I had suspected.

## SUDDENLY A PROMOTION

A short while after, the director of my department called me in and asked me to take an examination for a higher position which was opening up. I felt that I was completely unqualified for this position and told him so. But he smiled reassuringly, said that he thought I was qualified and urged me not to fail to take the test. I was so convinced that I wasn't qualified for the job that I almost decided not to show up; but, because of his urging, I went.

Expecting a room full of men competing for so important a job,

**65**

I was surprised when I arrived to find that only two others were taking the test with me. I was given the examination paper and told to turn it face down on my desk until time for the examination to begin. When we were told to begin and I looked over the test, I was *amazed* at the simplicity of the questions. I thought, "Is this all there is to it? I'm sure glad the boss insisted that I come!"

I finished my paper quickly and easily. The other two men continued to struggle with theirs and were still working when the examiner told them to stop. We were told to turn our papers face down on the desks and leave, for time had expired. He said we would be notified later as to how we had done. I left thinking about how easy the test had been and wondering why the other two had seemed to have such a difficult time with it.

I went directly to the office and the director was waiting for me. He met me at the door, stuck out his hand and said, "Congratulations, Jim, you got the promotion! You were the only one who knew all the answers. You will soon be called to take an 'on-the-job' training course, and then you can start on your new job."

He shook my hand again and went back to his office. I was pleased but a little bewildered. I still could not understand how it had been so easy and *how* could he know so soon that I was selected? Why, the ink was barely dry on my paper!

With questions about this still whispering in my mind, but mostly just excited and happy, I hurried home at the end of the day to tell Bonnie. She was, of course, delighted too. In light of her good job, plus my promotion, we decided to move out of the duplex apartment and buy our own home. We were making progress!

## BUT UNCLE IRVIN WASN'T PLEASED

I called Uncle Irvin to tell him the good news about my being in the Scottish Rite. I thought he would be pleased and proud. But he didn't seem pleased or proud of me at all. He appeared to resent it, envious of my being a 32nd Degree Mason.

He said that he had never been allowed to enter the Rite, and went on to explain, "Even though I was Past Master of my Lodge, I couldn't go in because there was a man in the Scottish Rite who didn't like me. He said that if I ever tried to enter he would 'blackball' me."

I was amazed, and asked, "Whatever became of 'Masonic brotherhood'?"

Uncle Irvin wouldn't answer my question, so I didn't tell him he had been lied to by that brother Mason. As long as a man is a Master Mason in good standing in his Blue Lodge, he *cannot* be blackballed and kept out of the Scottish Rite.

## THE RAISING OF MIKE AND THE "HANDS-OFF POLICY"

Working with me on the same shift was a man named Mike. He was a Scotsman with a wonderful accent, a warm heart and a somewhat quick temper. He was not very tall, but very solidly built and strong as a bull. He had been badly injured as a fireman in New York City and, after a long time in the hospital, had retired from the Fire Department. He had come to Florida, found work with the civil service of our large city, was assigned to my department, and we had become friends. Mike knew that I was a Mason (I had spoken to him about it from time to time), and one day he told me that he would like to be a Mason too. I, of course, was pleased, and asked him if he would like to belong to my Lodge. He said that was exactly what he wanted, so I got a petition and had another man (who worked with us) to sign it with me. Mike was duly investigated, approved, and was soon ready to take the degrees.

As I was now Senior Deacon, I was the one to conduct candidates through the initiations. I was pleased that I was going to get to lead my friend through. It happened that Mike was the only man going through at that time so things moved along smoothly and quickly. I had a pretty easy time of it. Until the latter part of the Third Degree.

Before we began that final night of Mike's Blue Lodge initiation, I spoke with the three men who were to portray the "three ruffians" Jubela, Jubelo, and Jubelum. I asked them to take it easy on Mike and explained why. They said they understood and would be gentle with him.

Everything went smoothly until we came to the part where I was leading Mike, as Hiram Abiff, to the "South Gate" where he was met by Jubela, the first "ruffian." As is always done, Jubela grabbed him and jerked him around a bit. It was gentle compared with what the candidate usually goes through, but it was too much for Mike, much too much, and he *erupted*! He pushed Jubela away, ripped off the hoodwink, roared like a mad bull and picked Jubela up! In one mighty motion, Mike threw him across the Lodge Hall. Jubela hit the black and white tiles and went sliding across the floor on his back, spinning slowly around and slid right up against the altar, which stopped him. He wasn't hurt badly, but lay there against the altar, not moving.

Mike had assumed a wrestler's stance, feet widespread, powerful arms at the ready, and bellowed out, "No mon puts his honds on me!" At first there was not a sound in the Lodge Hall, except for Mike. He stood there, looking slowly around the room, glaring at the brothers assembled, and continued to roar, "No mon puts his honds on me!"

Suddenly the Lodge was in an uproar. Some of the brothers convulsed with laughter, some were shouting excitedly at one another and some sat still in stunned silence. Mike was still standing there, challenging them all, and continuing to roar, "No mon puts his honds on me!" This scene in the sacred Hall was unprecedented, unheard of, *unthinkable!*

Many of the brothers were looking at the Worshipful Master, expecting him to "do something"; but he wasn't any more ready to "do something" about Mike than was Jubela the ruffian, who was still lying quietly against the altar. The Master just sat there, still as a statue in his black top hat, looking straight ahead.

I tried to calm Mike down but had no effect at all on him. I then went over to consult with the Worshipful Master. I tried to explain and told him that if I could take Mike out to the Preparation Room I thought I could calm him down and we would be able to proceed. He nodded his head and continued to sit there as if stunned, not moving.

I went back to Mike, who was still turning slowly from side to side in the center of this sudden storm, and spoke again with him.

He agreed to go out with me. We closed the Lodge Hall door behind us. In the Preparation Room Mike began to relax some and I told him I was really sorry about what had happened and would try to work it out so that we could proceed with his initiation. He just said, "All right Jim — but *no* mon puts his honds on me."

I left Mike in the Preparation Room and went back out to consult again with the Worshipful Master. I told him I thought it would be best to leave out Jubelo and Jubelum and just have Mike lie down on the canvas and let them bury him. The Master looked at me strangely and then asked, "Forever?"

Since that was all the Master said, I took it that my compromise solution was acceptable, so I returned to the Preparation Room. I explained to Mike the whole scene and what was going to happen. I told him that if he would just let us do the rest of it, gently, it would soon be over and he would be a Master Mason. He agreed, but firmly repeated the admonition, "No mon puts his honds on me."

So we went back into the Lodge Hall, let him lie down on the canvas and completed his initiation, albeit considerably modified. Mike never lived down that night and for many years jokes were made about Mike and the "Honds-Off Policy."

## I BECOME A DEGREE MASTER

The Master of the 25th Degree in the Scottish Rite moved to California. I was appointed to replace him. I got from him the degree book and, although it was not required of me, memorized the entire degree (the ritual and lesson to be taught or performed in that degree). It was to be exemplified (put on in full, as a dramatization) at the next Reunion. I was determined to do it better than it had ever been done.

Mike and I continued to be friends, becoming closer. With my encouragement he soon came into the Scottish Rite with me; since it is the "Scottish" Rite it seemed to me that we should have at least one Scotsman. Since by that time I was Master of the 25th Degree, I appointed Mike Orator. With his heavy Scottish accent, he seemed the perfect choice. I gave him his part and had him memorize it. When I told him he would have to wear a pasted-on artificial beard he decided just to grow his own, and he did.

When Reunion came around we were ready. It all went perfectly. The Secretary was so pleased with the way we exemplified the degree that he thanked and congratulated us all, making all the hard work and rehearsing worth it. We had not just "gotten by," we had done it better than anyone could remember its ever having been done before.

## FILLING THE VOID

As I had said to the incoming Worshipful Master when asking him to consider me for "a chair" in the Blue Lodge, I had no intention of just settling down and getting comfortable. Looking back on it all, I'm really not sure why I was so eager to get to the higher offices and to do it so soon. I am sure it was not just prideful ambition, or a desire for recognition. It was something much more valid and substantial, some need down deep inside of me.

Having grown up with no religious training, no church affiliation of any kind, and no spiritual identity, I really had no concept of the meaning of life. I had no philosophy nor any basic view of life, death and eternity. And, without realizing it at first, this emptiness in my life was being filled with what I was learning and doing in Masonry.

From the very beginning I had been troubled by the fact that so many of the men just came to Lodge and sat there. When the Master rapped, they stood up; when he rapped again, they sat down. When he said anything that called for a vote, they said "So mote it be," and when the meeting came to an end they got up and went home. Some had to be awakened and told it was time to leave. Many were members for many years, and always sat in the same seat. I was determined not to be such a "seat warmer"; I wanted to function, to learn all that there was to learn. I wanted to grow, and that was exactly what I was doing — at last.

## A CHAPLAIN LEARNS TO PRAY

In the Scottish Rite I became acquainted with the undertaker who had knocked me out with the setting maul when I was initiated into the Third Degree. He was to be the new Venerable Master of the Lodge of Perfection (one of the Four Bodies and the one in which all business meetings are held).

I hadn't seen him for a while and told him of my appointment as Senior Deacon in the Blue Lodge. I then told him that I would like to be an officer in the Lodge of Perfection, if he had room for me, and he said he would keep me in mind.

I realize that this may sound a little pushy, but actually it wasn't; it is not at all easy for incoming Masters to get men to volunteer for offices and they usually appreciate such willingness.

As is the case in all walks of life, most want the "honor" of belonging, but do not want to do the work. I didn't know what to expect from him, but when he assumed office he appointed me Chaplain.

At last I was finding a place for myself; I was an officer in both the Blue Lodge and the Scottish Rite. But there was a problem — a big one; as Chaplain I was going to have to pray and I didn't know how. I had not been in church since the last time my grandmother had taken me and knew nothing of prayer. I had heard the prayers from the ritual in the Lodge, but couldn't remember any of them. I asked the new Venerable Master about praying and he eased my mind some. He said that he would give me two cards with the opening and closing prayers printed on them and that I could simply read them out loud. But he also said that I would be expected to "give prayers" at banquets and at the assembling of the Scottish Rite Guard. So I would have to get an idea of how to pray and what prayers to use. There was no way around it. I was going to have to learn to pray.

We had a new man in the incoming class at the Blue Lodge who was pastor of the Methodist Church next door to the Lodge Hall. I called on him and told him I was the new Chaplain in the Lodge of Perfection and that I needed to know something about prayer. He said he would help me and the next day when I looked in my mail box I found a book called "The Prayers of John Wesley."

I studied the book and then wrote out several of the prayers, just as they were in the book, just as Wesley wrote them. I thought they were really good and felt that I was at last prepared for my new office. Whenever I was called upon to pray, I could just read one of those prayers out loud. I was ready — or so I thought.

At the next assembling of the Scottish Rite Guard (for the opening of the initiation of a new class at Reunion) I gave the prayer while the Guard of 25 men stood. It was one of the prayers of John Wesley I had taken from the book.

I thought the prayer was first rate and felt good about it; but when the opening ceremony was finished the Commander of the Guard called me aside and rebuked me sharply. He said, "You kept my men standing at attention for five whole minutes!" He also called me a "religious fanatic" and said that it was bad enough I kept the men standing five minutes, but *then* I had ended the prayer "in Christ's holy name." For *that,* he said, I would be *reported!* I was stung by his rebuke, especially since I had worked so hard to get it right and had no idea I was doing anything wrong.

I said since he was so rude to me I didn't care what he thought, that I didn't know anything about his 30-second prayers, and that from that time on he could say them himself!

As I walked away, I thought, "Some brother *he* is, to speak to me like that! At least he could have left out that part about 'religious fanatic' since I don't even know what prayers are except for the ones on the cards and in the book."

Very soon after, I was called in to see the Secretary of the Scottish Rite about my unsatisfactory performance. He was nice about it, but told me that I was *never* to end a prayer "in Jesus' name" or "in Christ's name." He said, "Make your prayers *universal.*"

I wondered about all this fuss over a prayer, especially one that came out of a book a preacher had lent me; but I just thanked him and left.

I was to learn the meaning and significance of this fuss over a prayer later on, [1] but for the time being I just accepted it. At least the Secretary was nice about it. Many years later, when he died, I learned that he was a Christian Scientist.

## INTO THE EASTERN STAR

Bonnie had supported and encouraged me in Lodge work from the start. As already stated, she had been an inactive member of the

Order of the Eastern Star when we were married, although I had not known it at the time. After my promotion, and as I became more and more active in Blue Lodge and the Scottish Rite, Bonnie told me one night that she intended to begin attending the Eastern Star and thought it would be good for me to join.

I agreed, submitted my application, and was soon approved and initiated. Many people believe that "The Star" is only for women, but it isn't.

The Order of the Eastern Star was conceived by a man, men organized it, men wrote the rituals, and no meeting can be held without at least three male officers present. Men, one might fairly say, control The Order of the Eastern Star, but only from the background.

The social life was pleasant, and now there was one meeting each week that Bonnie and I could attend together.

Although I could have been an officer in the Eastern Star, I had no desire to be. I had plenty to do already in the Blue Lodge and Scottish Rite and I was content just to enjoy going with Bonnie to the meetings and the social functions that went with them.

## THE KORAN, FEZ, AND FUN:
### BECOMING A SHRINER

The Shrine (Ancient Arabic Order, Nobles of the Mystic Shrine) is easily the most conspicuous of all forms of Freemasonry and the most far-removed from basic Masonic principles and traditions. Many who know nothing of Masonry in general who perhaps don't even recognize the word "Mason" except for thinking it means some kind of bricklayer, have at least a vague awareness of "The Shriners."

At the mention of the word "Shriner" most will think of men in red hats with tassels, perhaps in colorful costumes, parading, clowning and doing some kind of public service.

If they are a little more aware than that, they will think of them as men who have big conventions and drink a lot. Most of the general public will go through life with no knowledge of the existence of the Scottish Rite or the York Rite; the degrees of these

Bodies and such titles as Prince Adept, Master of the Royal Secret or Knight Templar will have no meaning at all for them.

They may never even have heard of the Blue Lodge and the degree of Master Mason. But they will probably have heard of the Shriners and will have some knowledge of what they do. The Shrine, the "Show Army of Masonry," maintains a *very* high profile.

I had been aware of the Shrine for a long time when I had only the most vague knowledge of the rest of Freemasonry. From the time of my very first entrance into the Lodge, I had the thought of someday being a Shriner. It seems to me that this is true of most Masons who go on beyond the Blue Degrees.

For this reason, one of their practices always puzzled me: after each Reunion in the Scottish Rite, the Shriners would come around, recruiting the new 32nd Degree Masons for the Shrine and it seemed unnecessary. Such was the case with me. Shortly after receiving the 32nd Degree they began approaching me about joining. In my case they were wasting their time, for I had decided a long time before to join them.

It is necessary to be a 32nd Degree Mason for six months before being eligible to join the Shrine. Unlike myself in a way, I didn't rush in as soon as the six months passed. I was fully involved in the Blue Lodge and already was an officer in the Scottish Rite; perhaps, also, I sensed that work in the Shrine wasn't as serious as in Blue Lodge and the Rite. I wanted to *learn* — about religions and the meaning of life — and I had plenty to learn where I was. So I didn't enter the Shrine after the Spring Reunion when I became eligible.

I was Chaplain in the Scottish Rite and a Degree Master. In the Blue Lodge I was Senior Deacon and preparing to be the Junior Warden, only two chairs away from the office of Worshipful Master. I was very busy with all this responsibility.

The following fall however, after Reunion, I decided it was time to enter the Shrine. Mike had come into the Scottish Rite at Spring Reunion and was now eligible also. We went into the Shrine together. I knew that the Shrine initiations got really rambunctious and wondered what might happen when they laid hands roughly on

Mike. The initiation was performed in the Coliseum before a very large crowd of Shriners who came to see the fun. One of the first things done was to identify the men with health problems that might make the initiation a risk.

There were physicians there to question and examine the candidates; those considered risky were separated out, had a white tape put around the left wrist, and they simply sat while the other candidates went through the rowdy part of it all. In this way, because of his previous back injury, Mike was spared the hazing and the Shrine was thus spared a demonstration of the "Honds-Off Policy."

We began the initiation about noon that Saturday. After the medical screening came the hazing, which was very childish. Some of it was not only childish, but downright vulgar. At one point we were placed in a large, mesh cage, and one of the Shriners climbed up on top of it. He exposed a very convincing rubber penis which was connected to a water bag concealed in his clothing and hosed down all of us in the cage to the delighted howls of the spectators.

After the hazing it was time for the serious part, the ritual, and then time to take the oath. We took the obligation, again with terrible bloody consequences if we revealed any of the "secrets" (one form of mayhem we promised to accept was to have our "eyeballs pierced to the center with a sharp, three-edged blade"). And, with the Koran on the altar, we sealed our solemn oath in the name of "Allah, the God of Arab, Moslem and Mohammedan, the God of our fathers." [2]

I had taken so many bloody oaths already (one for each degree) that I paid little attention to this one, except to notice that it, like the rest of the ritual, featured desert settings, Arabs and Allah, the Mohammedan god. I was disappointed and a little offended at the childish and vulgar nature of the initiation but not really surprised. This, after all, was the Shrine; and "fun" was the Shriners' trademark.

The initiation was completed by 4 p.m., so we could all be ready for the big celebration banquet that night. With still another initiation behind me, I headed home to share the moment with Bonnie and to get ready for the celebration. It was to be a BYOB ("bring your own bottle") affair, Mike was going with us, and we were looking forward to wearing our brand-new fezes. We enjoyed the party, which lasted until 2 a.m.; we were Shriners at last and it felt good.

There was no "degree work" in the Shrine for there is no actual degree, so it didn't look like I would be learning a great deal there. However, I looked forward to being a part of all their benevolent community services. I was proud of my new red fez with its gold trim and tassel.

I didn't see how my life could be much more full — except for one thing. I still had a spiritual emptiness; I was still in search of a religion.

### Footnotes

[1] *In a well-ordered lodge, Jesus is never mentioned except in vague, philosophical terms. Prayers are never prayed in His name, and when scriptures are quoted in the ritual, all references to Him are simply omitted. For example, II Thessalonians 3:6 is used in the ritual, but not the way it is in your Bible; the words "in the name of our Lord Jesus Christ" are entirely omitted. Likewise, the ritual includes I Peter 2:5, but with the words "by Jesus Christ" omitted. Albert Mackey, after Albert Pike the highest Masonic authority, calls this changing of the scriptures "a slight but necessary modification" (Masonic Ritualist, pg.272)*

[2] *Every Shriner, kneeling before the Koran, takes this oath in the name of Allah, and acknowledges this pagan god of vengeance as his own ("the God of our fathers"). And, in the ritual, he acknowledges Islam, the declared blood-enemy of Christianity, as the one true path. ("Whoso seeketh Islam earnestly seeks true direction.") How it must break the heart of God to hear these words from the lips of His own children, particularly the leaders of His church.*

# Chapter 8

# A RELIGION AT LAST

As I continued my progression "through the chairs," from office to higher office in the Blue Lodge, I also continued to work in more and more of the Scottish Rite degrees. As I continued to study in the degree rituals and lectures, I developed more and more of a clear understanding of religious beliefs and moved ever closer to a personal religious belief of my own.

## "THE LODGE IS A GOOD ENOUGH RELIGION"

Through the years I must have heard hundreds of men say, "I don't need to go to church — the Lodge is a good enough religion for me." So very many such men never attend a church except with the Lodge once a year to hear Masonry exalted. They trust Lodge membership and their own "virtuous life" to assure them acceptance in the "Celestial Lodge above."

In a sense I agreed with such men, in that I believed that the churches and synagogues knew and taught only imperfect remnants and perversions of the "old religions," the ancient mystery religions of the East. But I was not in agreement with them in another sense: I was not going to be satisfied with basing my life on

77

anything so vague. I was going to continue the search until I had a specific, foundational religious belief. And I wasn't there yet.

## The Ten Commandments

Still motivated in my search for religious understanding, I was happy when asked to become Master of the 18th Degree. In this degree, the Degree of the Rose Croix, I read that "The ceremonies of this degree are interpreted by each individual according to his own faith, for in no other way can Masonry retain its universal character."

The degree book went on to say that the symbolism for this degree comes from the "ankh," the Egyptian symbol for life, which comes from Deity (God), meaning that the Egyptian gods were at least the equal of the Christian God. It also said that "In all religions there is a basis of truth; in all there is pure morality."

As I read these words I thought they sounded wonderful. I didn't stop to realize that this endorsement of "all religions" included all cruel forms of paganism with mutilation and human sacrifices, voodoo, witchcraft (which often refers to itself as "The Old Religion") and all forms of Satanism. The degree book tied all this together by saying that Masonry has the mission of bringing together "all men of all religions" under the Masonic banner and around the Masonic altar.

The degree also features the Ten Commandments, which I thought particularly nice, and in performing this part of the ritual one day a very important insight came to me.

## A Disturbing Thought

At the next Reunion this Degree of Rose Croix was exemplified. I had my team well prepared for the performance. I was feeling good about it—not only the "truth" I thought I was expressing, but also the effective way we were performing the ritual. One of the candidates in the class of initiates was the mayor of our large city, a very important man and, in a way, my boss. As usual, one of the men in the class was selected to actually participate, representing the rest; we chose, of course, His Honor, the mayor.

At the end of the oath I had him kneeling at the altar, I had the Book of the Law in my hand, and he was vowing to keep the Ten

Commandments. As I read each one from the book, he repeated it after me and promised to keep it. About half way through the Commandments the thought occurred to me, "You cannot possibly do what you are promising to do. I know you, and know something of your life, and you cannot keep these Commandments. As a matter of fact, I don't think I know *anyone* who *could*."

Nevertheless, the mayor promised with a terrible oath, "So mote it be." This interesting contradiction stayed with me, returning to my thoughts from time to time. The vast majority of men administering and taking the oath, however, seem only to say it, get it over, and promptly forget it.

## 1 BECOME WORSHIPFUL MASTER

When my time came to be elected Worshipful Master of the Blue Lodge I had to stop taking on extra responsibilities in the Scottish Rite. I was already working in four degrees, plus my participation in the Eastern Star and Shrine. Serving as Worshipful Master takes most of the "spare time" one has, for the duties are demanding. Of course, I had the full cooperation of my superiors at my job, for they were Masons and were pleased with what I was doing. They gave me plenty of time off for Masonic funerals and other extra activities, and this was never a problem.

## AN INTERESTING TESTIMONY

On the evening after my installation as Master we had a special dinner party for the outgoing Master. It was very nice, with a private party room in a large hotel, complete with its own bar. During the party we asked the outgoing Master to share with us the story of how he had entered Masonry and his progression in it. He had already had quite a bit to drink and was very frank in the telling of his "testimony" as a Mason.

We laughed as he told us that when he applied for membership he was amazed that the Investigating Committee approved him for membership. He said, "I could hardly believe that they were telling me I was approved, for I was so drunk when they arrived that I couldn't get up. My wife had to let them in, for even if I had been able to get up on my feet I could not have taken the chance of walking across the room and falling down."

I laughed with everyone else at first. Then I was troubled by the obvious contradiction there. One of the basic tenets of Masonry is *sobriety*. Yet this Past Master was accepted for membership when so drunk he couldn't stand up and walk. This troubling thought, like the one about the Ten Commandments, stayed with me.

## A STRANGE AND INTERESTING THEORY

We had regular luncheons at the Acacia Club, for Masons only. We would usually have a drink at the bar, then go into the club room and have lunch. After lunch we always had a speaker.

One such speaker was a Methodist preacher, a dedicated Mason and a student of the Ancient Mysteries. He had a strange and interesting theory to the effect that Masonry was actually founded by Nimrod at the building of the Tower of Babel. Of course I knew nothing of the Bible, so accepted everything he said as truth.

Now that I have made a study of the Scriptures I know that they teach no such thing. However, having also learned much of the dark and shadowy origins of Masonry, I realize that the strange preacher may not have been so far from the truth.

## I WANTED TO UNDERSTAND

My year as Worshipful Master of the Blue Lodge was a pleasant experience. I enjoyed the work in the weekly meetings and bringing classes through the first three degrees. It was also nice being treated with such respect and being called "Worshipful" and "Master."

Because the office required so much of my time and energy, my thoughts were once more really focused on the Blue Lodge (rather than on the Scottish rite degrees and the Shrine work). I had questioned things almost from my beginnings in Masonry, not that I was skeptical, but because I wanted so much to learn and to understand. I wasn't satisfied just to sit through it, say it and get it over with; I wanted to *learn*. Masonry was giving meaning to my life, and I wanted to *grasp* it *all*.

## WHAT IS A COWAN?

I remembered a question that occurred to me during one of the very first lectures I heard. It was about Masonic origins and the lecturer said that the name "Blue Lodge" came from "our ancient brethren who met on the high hills and low vales at night, meeting under the starry canopy of Heaven," the blue sky. The lecture went on to say that the ancient brethren set guards "to keep off cowans and eavesdroppers."

My mind grabbed onto the word "cowan," as I had never heard it before. After the meeting I asked the Tiler (the officer in the Lodge responsible for guarding the door and keeping cowans and other "profane" persons out of the hall) what a cowan is. Since it was his duty to keep them out, I assumed that he would know what they were.

He looked puzzled, and finally said, "I think it is a no-good bum." So I asked about a dozen other men (including all the officers) the same question that night and no one could tell me what a cowan is.

Many years later I finally learned that it is an old term for an untrained builder of walls who hadn't the knowledge of stone masonry and who in the middle ages could be found eavesdropping on meetings of builders' guilds, trying to learn their secrets.

This questioning became a pattern in my life as a Mason. It sometimes got me in trouble but it also made me a much better-informed Mason than most. Had anyone asked me, when I was Worshipful Master, what a "cowan" was, I could have answered the question. But no one ever asked.

## THE JUNIOR WARDEN LEAVES THE LODGE

While I was Worshipful Master the man who was Junior Warden asked me one day about the Bible. He pointed out that in the ritual we say that the Bible is a "rule and guide for faith and practice" and that it teaches that the Christian God is the only true one and that Jesus is the only means of salvation.

Yet, he reminded me, we teach in the Lodge that all religions are valid. He pointed out to me that there is a contradiction there and asked me to explain it to him. When I couldn't do it he left the Lodge and renounced Masonry. I thought he was a bit extreme but never forgot the question. This man had been a dedicated Mason and a hard worker in the Lodge, only two chairs away from being Worshipful Master. He left it all for Jesus and the Bible.

## MORE QUESTIONS WITHOUT ANSWERS

With the closing of my year as Worshipful Master I returned to the work in the Scottish Rite with all my might. I studied more of the degrees, studied the references in "Morals and Dogma" and other sources and continued to ask questions. As before, my questions continued to be met with annoyed silence or advice to "Stop asking questions that have no answer and just follow the Ritual." I asked so many questions the Secretary finally had a special meeting of the officers to deal with the "problem" I was creating.

When they told me that my questions had no answers and that I should be satisfied just to follow the books, I said my piece. I told that body of officers that I believed the answers *were* there but that no one *cared* enough to find them.

For example, I wanted to know why we were called "Scottish" Rite, when the degrees and the system originated in France. "Why not call it the French Rite?" I asked. Again there was no answer, and the conference concluded with, "Just stick to the Ritual and stop trying to write your own opinions into the system. It *is* Scottish, no matter what anyone else may say."

In spite of the special meeting's conclusions, several of the officers approached me later and asked how I had learned these things that were so disturbing. I gladly shared with them my irrefutable Masonic sources and they seemed to be taking it all in. But it didn't change anything. Their interest was only mild and temporary. They had no real desire to know the truth.

I began to realize that there are two classes of Masons: one that just sits through the meetings; and the other that does the work, but just keeps to the Ritual and memorizes or reads it without understanding.

I really didn't fit into either category but was still blind to the Bible and its truth. So I kept on asking. I continued searching for answers in the degrees and other writings of the Masonic authorities.

## A KNIGHT COMMANDER OF THE COURT OF HONOR

In spite of the fact that I was "making waves" with all my questioning and seeking for understanding, I continued to make real progress in the Rite and to accumulate honors and recognition. There is a special honor, beyond the 32nd Degree, called "Knight Commander of the Court of Honor" (K.C.C.H.). With the lifetime title goes a special red cap with the K.C.C.H. emblem.It was a happy day when I was notified that I had been selected (by the 33rd Degree representatives) to receive this high honor.

In order to receive the K.C.C.H. it was necessary for me to travel to a distant city. Since Bonnie was working she was not able to go along, so Mike said he would go with me. We were given time off from our jobs to make the trip (our superiors were pleased about it all) even though it wasn't necessary for Mike to go. We took the train to the Conclave, and it was a pleasant trip. I was excited and Mike was happy for me.

There was a great deal of drinking at the Conclave and it bothered me. "Why must we *always* do so much drinking?" I asked myself, but had no answer. I enjoyed a little drinking and did it regularly. But it bothered me that there was always so *much* of it and that it played such a major role in the Masonic life. I received the Honor and we enjoyed a banquet after the ceremony. The next morning there was a meeting in the Lodge Hall and a lecture was given by the Grand Master of the Grand Lodge of Florida, a very prominent Mason. I felt honored by all of it.

That afternoon Mike and I took the train back home. As we reflected on it all, he said that he hoped he could become a K.C.C.H. someday and I said that was my hope also. Bonnie was glad to see me, was proud of the honor I had received, and thought I looked distinguished in my snappy new red cap.

## A RELIGIOUS BELIEF AT LAST

It was time again to be getting ready for Reunion and there was much to be prepared as I was now working in four degrees at once. As I studied more and more, I saw with increasing clarity that Masonry teaches that whatever a man sincerely and conscientiously believes is truth, and that all religions are of equal worth and validity. Thus, Jesus Christ is reduced to the level of the other "exemplars" such as Buddha, Mohammed, Confucius, Pythagoras and Emmanuel Swedenborg.

Albert Mackey wrote (in The Masonic Ritualist), "Thus the trestleboard (blueprint for life) of the Jew is the Old Testament, of the Mohammedan the Koran; the Veda Scriptures of Hinduism and the writings of Baha-ullah are just as good as the Word of the Christians' God, for the fact is that all religions are never as good as the pure teachings of Freemasonry."

Albert Mackey, that eminent Masonic leader and philosopher who believed that all the religions of man are of equal validity, but are inferior to the "pure teachings of Masonry," also believed in reincarnation. As a matter of fact, Mackey believed that in one of his previous lives on earth he had been Jacques DeMolay, the medieval soldier crusader who was burned at the stake in France for betraying the faith and victimizing pilgrims in the Holy Land.[1]

## A SERIOUS CONTRADICTION

Of course, there are immediate problems here because many of these religious systems that are "all correct" or of "equal validity" claim to be the *only* valid and correct one. So it becomes obvious that they cannot all be "right" or of equal validity. But my mind was not prepared to see this serious contradiction. I accepted this idea that it doesn't really matter what you believe as long as you are sincere. To undergird and hold together this unsubstantial assortment of contradictory beliefs, there was the theory of reincarnation.

As Mike and I finished up the degree work in still another Reunion, we discussed the lecture he gave in the 25th Degree and the one I gave in the 32nd Degree. Neither of us had ever studied the Bible. No one had ever witnessed to us plainly about Jesus as the Redeemer, and so we decided that we would find the truth about religion in the degrees. Mike had been a Catholic in Scotland, but had left all that behind when he came to America. He said, "I don't want any more to do with Christianity."

## WE EMBRACE REINCARNATION

With the degree work and other Masonic writings as our source, we finally decided that the truth lay in reincarnation and that if we would try to live a good life now, be good to our brother Masons, help the sick and attend to good deeds in general, when we died we would enter the next life on a higher plane — just like going through a door. However, if we did not try to live right and do well in this life, then we could expect to go through that door into a lower form of life, perhaps as a barbarian in the Dark Ages, or a poor wretch living in ignorance and poverty in the Far East.

We remembered, for example, the exemplification of the 31st degree. In this degree the candidate, as a typical man who has just died, is defending his life before the gods and goddesses of Egypt. The candidate tells of his good works in his just-ended life and of his hope for a better incarnation in the next. As the candidate tells of each work he has done, one of the Egyptian deities drops a stone into the pan of a scale. As the last stone is dropped into the pan by the god Anubis (a man with a ram's head), the scale tips and Osiris and Isis, who are presiding, say, "Weighed in the balance and found wanting." The candidate listens then as the Soul of Cheres, symbol of immortality, is brought before the Chamber of the Dead and he learns that he must improve in his next life in order to advance in the cycle of reincarnation.

## A DUAL COMMITMENT

So we decided to accept the doctrine of reincarnation and made a dual commitment. We made a commitment to the concept as a religious belief. We also made a commitment to one another to do the best we could in this life so as to be together on a higher plane in the next. We examined all the evidence at our disposal, made a decision, and then a sincere commitment to try to live up to it.

Mike and I thought that somehow, by accepting reincarnation and doing the best we could, we would someday find ourselves together in that "Grand Lodge on High."

Bonnie really didn't agree with us concerning reincarnation but didn't say much about it. She seemed to know something, way down deep, that we didn't know. But she didn't object to our decision and commitment and we pressed on.

At last, I had a religion of my own! I had the religion of Masonry (the Egyptian Mystery Religion of Isis and Osiris) with its undergirding doctrine of reincarnation and the Lodge really was "a good enough religion for me."

## Footnote

[1]*The Order of Demolay, Masonic organization for boys too young to enter the Lodge, is named for Jaques DeMolay, regarded in Masonic tradition as a hero.*

# Chapter 9

# CHE GACHERING SCORM

With a religion of my own, at last, I entered into a period of four satisfying years. It was a time of steady, single-minded work and accomplishment, a stable period of progress. In my work in the Scottish Rite, especially, they were years of fulfillment. But with the satisfaction of the work and the learning, there were some disappointments and a measure of disillusionment.

## DISAPPOINCMENC IN CHE SHRINE

Soon after becoming a K.C.C.H., I spoke to the Illustrious Potentate of the Shrine about the possibility of my "moving up" to the office of Illustrious Potentate. I was working in the Shrine as much as my responsibilities in the Scottish Rite and Blue Lodge would allow. As a matter of fact, I was one of the hardest workers in our Shrine Lodge. I had become one of that committed few upon whom the Potentate depended to keep things going. Every organization, it seems, has such people who do most of the work.

## YOU DON'C QUALIFY

When I told him I was interested in becoming "Illustrious Potentate" someday (this office, like that of Worshipful Master in the Blue Lodge, is held for only one year), I thought he would be pleased — that he would encourage me to seek it.

Instead, he looked at me a moment and then said, "Jim, you can never expect to be Illustrious Potentate in the Shrine. The office requires someone with more money and a nicer house than you have. This office requires entertaining visiting Potentates and other important people and you would not be able to do that properly. You may as well forget it."

This really took me by surprise and it hurt my feelings. Once again, I saw a sharp contrast between the seriousness and depth of the Blue Lodge and Scottish Rite and the shallow, social and public relations emphases of the Shrine.

## THE ALL-STAR FOOTBALL GAME

Another disappointment came as I continued to work hard in the Shrine. I was appointed to a demanding and responsible job in connection with the All-Star Football Game we sponsored in order to raise money to build and operate our burn centers and hospitals for children. I was responsible for all arrangements for lodging, feeding and entertaining the coaches, players and others involved in putting on the game itself.

I was saddened and disillusioned by the vast amount of money that was spent on accommodations and entertainment for all these people, rather than going into the hospitals themselves. It really troubled me. But I soon learned that there was nothing I could do about it. So I just did my job and took comfort in the money that *did* go into the building and operation of the hospitals. But I couldn't forget it and it continued to trouble me.

## MASTER OF ALL SCOTTISH RITE BODIES

I went on working diligently in the Scottish Rite degrees, learning more and more about the "Old Religion" that had become my own, and believing that I was growing spiritually. During the next four years I continued to work in still more degrees, to make occasional waves by asking questions (which still went largely unanswered) and to gather recognition and honors.

By the end of this time I had become, in succession, Master of all four of the Scottish Rite Bodies and served as such with success and satisfaction. I had become, without seeking to be, the man generally looked upon as the outstanding leader in the Rite — the one most likely to "really amount to something."

Except for all my questioning and seeking for knowledge and understanding, I maintained harmonious and friendly relationships with all in the system. I was a little "hard-nosed" in my insistence on getting the job done, maintained a no-nonsense attitude about the work and demanded excellence of those working with me. But it was all positive, except for a few lazy ones I wouldn't tolerate, and the results were consistently good.

By becoming Master of all four Bodies I had accomplished something seldom done. I felt good thinking of how much I had learned in the process and had satisfaction, both in the sense of jobs well done and of growing in my religion. I had my roots down deep in the "Ancient Mystery Religions," was depending upon reincarnation and my good works to eventually get me into that "Celestial Lodge on High" and I was growing rapidly in terms of responsibility and accomplishment in the Lodge. I felt good about it all, and wondered how it could be any better. I soon found out.

## GOOD NEWS AND BAD NEWS

Fall Reunion was a hard but good one with a large class of candidates coming through. At the end of Reunion I was told that I was being considered for the 33rd Degree.

The 33rd Degree! This was almost too good to be real! I was K.C.C.H. and Past Master of all Scottish Rite Bodies and that was a lot of success and honor for one who had been an abandoned little boy. The thought that I might also be given the 33rd Degree made my head swim.

The 33rd Degree cannot be earned or bought. As a matter of fact, it cannot even be sought, for to ask for or seek it means automatic and permanent disqualification for the honor.

The Supreme Council of the 33rd Degree, seated in Washington, D.C. at the House of the Temple, reaches down and selects those it chooses. Except for a seat on the Supreme Council itself, this honor is the end of the line — there is none higher. Not only that, I had been a K.C.C.H. for only four years. A man cannot even be considered for the 33rd Degree until he has been a K.C.C.H. four years. I was being *considered* for the 33rd in the minimum time!

I was told that in about six months I would be notified as to whether I would actually be granted the 33rd. I thought, even if I were not selected, what an honor it was even to be considered!

Along with this almost unbelievably good news I began to notice a problem in my work and increasing difficulty on the job. In my work with the Port Authority I needed to be able to see names and numbers of ships and boats at a distance. Rather quickly, this became a problem. No matter how hard I tried, I noticed I could not read the names and numbers clearly from a distance as I had always been able to do.

Thinking I only needed to get some glasses that would solve the problem, I went to see an optician. He examined me and said he had bad news for me. He couldn't help me with the problem by prescribing glasses for distant vision. As a matter of fact, he said that he couldn't help me at all. He said that I had a progressive cataract developing on my left eye and would need to see a physician.

## A DOCTOR WITH SIMPLE GOOD NEWS

I went home and told Bonnie what had happened. She said she knew of an ophthalmologist she could recommend. This doctor had helped a lady she knew and she felt that he was the one I should see. This recommendation of Bonnie's was perhaps the most important turning point in my life. Of course I had no way of knowing it at the time. Simply doing what seemed the logical thing at the time, and with not the slightest inkling of the importance of what I was doing, I called his office and made an appointment.

## A BOLD DIAGNOSIS

When the day arrived I went to the doctor's office. My time came and I went into the examining room to wait for my pupils to dilate. The doctor came in, spoke with me briefly and began to examine my eyes. In what seemed to be a very short time, he completed his examination and then proceeded to give me a bold and startling diagnosis.

This man looked as if he were looking right through me for a moment and then said, "Mr. Shaw, it is true. You do have a developing cataract on your left eye, and there is one coming on your right eye also; but while your physical vision is bad, that isn't your real problem. Your real problem is with your spiritual vision."

I sat there feeling a strange kind of emotional impact, wondering what he meant.

Before I could ask, he spoke again with the same powerful simplicity and asked, "Mr. Shaw, are you saved?"

This time I did reply, and I asked him, "Saved from what?"

He said, "I mean, have you ever received the Lord Jesus Christ as your Savior and made Him the Lord of your life?"

By this time I was regaining my usual ability to carry on such verbal exchanges and, with a religious haughtiness rising up within me, I said to him, "Sir, I know more about religion than you do — as a matter of fact I know more about religion than most people will *ever* know!"

But he was neither impressed nor taken aback by my proud declaration. Without taking his eyes from mine or changing his expression he asked me, "But what do you know about *salvation?*"

Suddenly I had no more spirit for this exchange. I sensed that I was up against something very powerful, and said quietly, "I will think it over and let you know" and left as quickly as I could.

## "HE IS A RELIGIOUS FANATIC"

I left the doctor's office and went to my boss's office. I knew that I had a serious problem with my eyes and thought that I may have another problem of a different kind — one that I definitely didn't understand.

I asked my boss if I could take a two-week leave. He said, "Sure, Jim" and I went home to call my half-brother in Indianapolis. He was a Mason also, and I thought he might give me some advice. I told him what had happened, what the doctor had said, and he quickly gave me his opinion.

"That man is a religious fanatic," he told me. "You take the next plane here and I will meet you at the airport. Then I'll take you to see *my* ophthalmologist." The next plane left at 9 o'clock the following morning and I was on it.

## "GO BACK HOME AND DO WHATEVER HE TELLS YOU"

"When I arrived in Indianapolis my half-brother was waiting. He told me that I had an appointment with his doctor for the next day and took me to his home to rest and wait. The following day the doctor there examined me and then asked me where I lived. I told him where I lived, and also what the other doctor had said about my eyes (I didn't mention what the other man had said about my *spiritual* vision).

He replied, "I will look the man up in our Register."

When he came back into the examining room he said to me, "Mr. Shaw, you have the very best medical facilities available to you in Florida, and the doctor who examined you there is one of the very best. My advice to you is to go straight home and do *whatever he says.*"

My brother wasn't at all pleased. I was feeling a strange combination of dread and excited anticipation. There seemed to be no alternative except to do as he said. But *what,* I wondered, would that strange and intense doctor in Florida tell me to do?

## INCREASING KNOWLEDGE AND GROWING DISCOMFORT

Back home, I made another appointment and went to see the doctor. There was an unexpected complication: I had an infection in my eyelids. He said that he would not be able to operate for at least six weeks. So I returned to work and went each week for the next six weeks to be treated for the infection. Each time when I went to see the doctor for examination and treatment, he spoke to me about God's plan of salvation and my need of Jesus as my personal redeemer. He spoke to me about the Lord and quoted verses of Scripture.

## SEARCHING THE SCRIPTURES

His speaking to me this way no longer offended me. The verses of Scripture he quoted seemed to go way down inside of me. Some of them seemed to explode down there, stirring things I could neither describe nor understand. I decided that I would look up the verses he spoke of and read them for myself. The more I thought of it the more strongly I wanted to do it.

I had no Bible to read except for the big one on the coffee table. Bonnie had bought it when we were married and said that it would be our "family Bible." But it had lain there all those years without being read. At last it was opened and I began to look up the verses the doctor quoted and read them in their context. They sounded good as I read them. I would go back and read some of them again and again.

As the weeks passed I would sometimes wake up in the night thinking about one of the verses, get up and go into the living room to read it from that big Bible. The Scriptures definitely spoke to me — to needs deep within me. I noticed that they continued to speak to me, reverberating with meaning, no matter how many times I had read them. Those Bible verses were different from anything I had ever read before. They seemed *alive*.

There was a definite conflict going on within me as the Scriptures collided in my understanding with the teachings of the Masonic authorities and philosophers. I could feel the clouds swirling in my mind and was vaguely troubled, but didn't try to understand it. I just continued to read the big Bible in the living room, listen to the doctor as he witnessed to me, and do my Lodge work as well as I possibly could.

## THE SCRIPTURES WERE SO SIMPLE!

I didn't try to sort it all out or understand it. But I did notice something that became clearer and clearer. In addition to the strange "life" I sensed in the Scriptures, I noticed how *simple* their message was compared with the complexity of the Masonic writings.

## THE CONFLICT COMES INTO FOCUS

I had the surgery on my left eye and it was successful. With new glasses I could see well with that eye and after two weeks I went back to work. The operation on the right eye was scheduled to be done in six months. As surely as my vision was coming into clearer focus after the surgery, so was the conflict between the teachings of the Bible and the teachings of Masonry. I was increasingly aware of this in general terms, but it became clear in specifics when I gave the 32nd Degree Lecture at the next Coronation.

## ONE OR THE OTHER WAS WRONG

I had been understudy for some time to the judge who gave the Lecture of the 32nd Degree before I began to give it myself. I had heard it or given it many, many times and knew it well. Reunion was coming up, and Mike and I were making preparations. I studied all of my work thoroughly — the 32nd Degree Lecture with particular care. As I studied the lecture, and when I delivered it to the new class of 32nd Degree Masons, I saw that there was a significant difference here. I saw for the first time how different from the teachings of the Bible was the lecture, this summing up of all the Masonic teachings the men had gone through in working up to this climactic degree. There was a difference there — one that could not be reconciled and I saw it clearly.

Either the "Old Religions" and the teachings of Masonry are right and the Bible is wrong, or the Bible is right and the "Old Religions" and Masonic teachings are wrong. Both could not be right. It was, I now saw clearly, that simple.

## ON A COLLISION COURSE WITH A CHOICE

With this fundamental conflict now clearly in focus in my understanding, I saw the long-range implications of it all. Masonry taught salvation by works, depending on one's own "virtuous life" to redeem him. The Bible teaches salvation by grace, depending on the perfect life of Jesus and His atoning death for us. Masonry teaches that Jesus is no greater than the other "exemplars" of history (such as Mohammed, Buddah, Aristotle or Joseph Smith), and was neither divine nor inspired. The Bible teaches that Jesus is God the Son, that He has always existed, and that no man can be reconciled to God the Father except through Him. [1] There is a choice to be made here—I saw this clearly—and I was on a collision course with that choice.

## SEEKING THE COUNSEL OF OTHERS

Seeing clearly the conflict and the choice it demanded, I began, discreetly, to seek the counsel of others. I spoke with Bonnie and Mike about it, and with a few other close friends. I even went to see the Methodist preacher who had lent me the book of John Wesley's prayers when I was made Chaplain of the Lodge of Perfection. He really wasn't much help. He was not a zealous Mason and seldom attended Lodge meetings, but had no intention of leaving the Lodge altogether. He wasn't going to make that kind of trouble for himself! No one seemed to understand as clearly as I did. Bonnie came close, but none of them really saw the conflict and the choice it demanded, probably because they had not been reading the Scriptures as I had.

## THE LIGHT BREAKS THROUGH

During one of my regular visits to the doctor after the operation on my left eye, I was sitting in one of his examination rooms, waiting for him to come to check me. I am very much inclined to read whenever I must wait, no matter how brief the waiting period, so I looked around to see what was in there that I might read until he came. There was not a thing in that room to read, except a Bible.

I picked it up, opened it to John's Gospel, and began to read again some of the verses I had read so many times in chapters one, three and four. Then, turning over to chapter six, I began to read verses I had not read before.

My eyes seemed to move quickly over the words of Jesus: "I am the bread of life; he that cometh to me shall never hunger; and he that believeth on me shall never thirst...him that cometh to me I will in no wise cast out...and this is the will of him that sent me, that every one which seeth the Son, and believeth on him, may have everlasting life: and I will raise him up at the last day."

## "HEY, DOC...IS THIS REALLY TRUE?"

Then my eyes beheld verse 47, "Verily, verily, I say unto you, he that believeth on me hath everlasting life."

In spite of all the verses and passages of Scripture I had already read, and for reasons probably known only to God, this verse reached down inside me and grabbed my heart. I was staggered with the simplicity of what it said and the power of what it did to me. Trumpet fanfares inside my head could not have more effectively locked my attention on that simple verse, or more clearly shown its importance to me. It was doing powerful things, both in my heart and in my understanding.

"Could it really be true," I wondered, "that it could *all* be so *simple?* Could this really be true?"

Without thinking about courtesy or propriety in a large doctor's office, I called out loudly, "Hey, Doc!"

When, after a few seconds, he looked into the room where I was sitting, I pointed to that verse and asked, "Is this really true?"

He looked at the page, read the verse my finger was on and said, "Sure. Yes, Jim, of course it's true."

## THIS TIME IT WAS REAL

When one has been exposed to Masonic religion and philosophy, with all its confusion, doubt and doubletalk, for as long as I had been, it is hard to believe the simple truth when finally confronted with it — even the living truth of the Bible.

After being really convinced of the truth of the "Old Religion" and the doctrine of reincarnation, after believing and teaching others that Jesus was neither divine nor unique, it is not at all simple or easy to accept the truth that He *is* divine *and* unique.

Even though the doctor had been quoting Scriptures to me for nearly six months, and I had been studying them myself, there had been much confusion within me about it all.

But the supernatural power of the words of God had been doing their work within me and the simple truth of this verse suddenly broke through the clutter of tangled concepts in my mind.

The light of Truth suddenly broke through the fog of confusion and doubt.

It was TRUE! It was really that simple and it was TRUE! I had told Doc on occasion before that I believed the verses he spoke of, but I really hadn't. Much of that time I had been playing mind games with him. Now I did — I really did! This time I wasn't playing any mind games; this time it was *real*.

## SOMETHING INSIDE ME CHANGED

With the realization that the simple message of John 6:47 is true, a dark power within me was broken, a door in my heart opened and light came flooding into me. I felt an overwhelming sense of gladness and sadness — a rush of mixed emotions swirling within me.

I didn't try to interpret what I was feeling, but it was definitely a breakthrough of truth. I really *knew* it was truth and I was never the same again. Something inside me had changed, something that opened my eyes to truth and error, and the change was permanent. I would see things differently from that day on.

## AN OPERATION, A PRAYER AND A HURRICANE

The time came for me to have the second operation, the one to remove the cataract on my right eye, and I went back into the hospital confident that it would turn out as well as the first one. I wasn't worried at all. When the operation was over and I was back in my room, someone came in and took me by the hand.

I couldn't see, for both eyes were bandaged. When I asked him who he was, he said that he was the doctor's pastor.

He said, "Mr. Shaw, I just came from the operating room. The doctor always prays for his patients, and he and I prayed for you — before and after the surgery."

His words penetrated clear to the center of me and shook my emotions loose. I had never before, to my knowledge, had anyone really pray for me, *never*, and I choked on the significance of it.

When I could speak again I said to him, "Sir, as soon as I get out of the hospital and am able, I will be at your church."

He squeezed my hand and left me to think about it all. It was an overwhelming experience but definitely a good one.

Before my recuperation was complete a hurricane approached and the hospital authorities were asking all patients who were able to leave to do so. I was making much more rapid recovery than had been expected, so I called Bonnie and asked her to come get me. As she drove me home, I told her that although people from the doctor's church had visited me and had prayed for me, not one person from the Lodge had been there to see me. She told me that she had announced to the Eastern Star members that I was having the surgery. But not a one of them had come. The contrast was clear and unmistakable.

The physical hurricane that was approaching was paralleled, if not exceeded, by the spiritual and emotional one building up inside of me.

Footnote

[1] See Appendix A, "Masonic Doctrine Versus Christian Doctrine."

# Chapter Ten

# INTO THE LIGHT

The hurricane came and went without any harm to us. But the one within me continued to gather force. It seemed strange, from my point of view, for all the people around me seemed calm. Even the doctor was no longer speaking much to me about the Lord, for I wasn't seeing him regularly. Bonnie was quietly supportive, but we really didn't say much about it. Mike and my other friends went on with life. It was "business as usual" around me, but definitely not that way inside of me.

## THE HIGHEST MASONIC DEGREE

Easter was approaching and one quiet morning I was at home recuperating from the second operation when the doorbell rang. It was a special delivery letter from the Supreme Council in Washington, notifying me that I had been selected for the 33rd Degree.

I could hardly believe it was true! This honor is one most Masons never even think of receiving. It was just too much, too far out of reach, beyond limits of reality. It was unreal to think I had actually been selected. It was an honor just to be considered for this ultimate degree and I had actually been *selected*, chosen by that small and powerful group, the Supreme Council of the 33rd Degree.

I called Bonnie to share the good news with her. In talking with her, I surprised myself by asking her if she thought I should accept it.

"What a strange thing to ask her," I thought. But before I could contemplate it she said, "Why, *sure* you should accept it. You have worked so hard for so long to get there — by all means you should accept it."

So I returned my acceptance immediately and began making plans for the trip.

## I MADE IT ON MY OWN

With plenty of time to reflect, I thought about my long climb up the mountain of Masonry in search of light. I thought about the odds against anyone's ever making it to the 33rd Degree. I realized that in my case the odds had been even greater. I had made it by hard work and dedication alone. Some men have an edge on selection because of their wealth, political power or prominence. I had none of these.

Like the day I had carried the man all the way to the top of "Shaw Hill" between Camp Butner and Raleigh, I had made it to the top of the Masonic mountain because I was willing to make the effort required and refused to quit. Thinking of this, I felt particularly good about it and wished my mother could know.

I had come a long way since leaving the front gate that terrible day so many years ago. I had come the distance with no help from Uncle Irvin. Who would have thought that the lonely walk, begun so many years ago by that frightened little 13-year-old boy, would have led to this point? I had reached the pinnacle — made it all the way to the top.

Some of the most prominent and influential men in the world would undoubtedly be there to participate when I was given this ultimate degree — for me — little Jimmy Shaw, who had gone to work at age five and made it alone since age 13. They would be there to give the 33rd Degree to *me*. It was really a bit difficult to take it all in.

## 3 DAYS AT THE MOUNTAIN TOP

In order to receive the 33rd Degree it was necessary to go to Washington, D.C. The initiation and related functions were to last three days.

Since Bonnie could participate in practically none of the things I would be doing each day, she decided not to go along. We were both excited as I made preparations to leave. But I was not as excited as I expected to be. The edge was taken off the excitement because, in me, it was mixed with a considerable amount of conviction. Way down deep there was a growing restlessness, an increasing conflict, produced by the things the doctor had been sharing and by all the Scripture I had been reading. Preparing to receive this "ultimate honor" was not as thrilling as it might otherwise have been.

## ARRIVING AT THE HOUSE OF THE TEMPLE

I flew into Washington National Airport and took a taxi to the House of the Temple on Northwest 16th Street. Upon arriving at the Temple I was met by a receptionist who asked if I were there to receive the 33rd Degree. I was surprised to find a woman in those sacred Masonic precincts, but said that I was and showed her my letter from the Supreme Council. She then told me that in order to receive the degree, I would be expected to make a "minimum donation" of a very large amount of money (at least it was a *very large* amount for me). This took me completely by surprise for there had not been a word about any such "minimum donation" in the letter sent me by the Supreme Council. I didn't carry that much money with me and had left my checkbook at home but was able to borrow the money from one of the other men and gave it to her. We candidates were all unhappy about this unpleasant surprise and grumbled to one another about it, but were not unhappy enough to forsake the degree over it. We were too close to the "top of the mountain" to turn back at that point.

## THE TEMPLE ITSELF

The House of the Temple is quite impressive — a bit awesome, really. Standing large, grey and silent on the east side of Northwest 16th Street, between "R" and "S" Streets, it looms very wide and tall from the curb. There is a huge expanse of granite pavement in front of it, including three levels of narrowing steps as the entrance is approached. Flanking the entrance are two Sphinx-like granite lions with women's heads, the neck of one entwined by a cobra and decorated with the "ankh" (the Egyptian symbol of life and deity).

Adorning the neck and breast of the other is an image of a woman, symbolic of fertility and procreation. In the pavement, just in front of the tall bronze doors, are two Egyptian swords with curved, serpentine blades and, between the two swords, brass letters, set into stone, saying, "The Temple of the Supreme Council of the Thirty-Third and Last Degree of the Ancient and Accepted Scottish Rite."

Over the tall, bronze doors, cut into the stone, is the statement, "Freemasonry Builds Its Temples in the Hearts of Men and Among Nations." [1]

High above the entrance, partially concealed by stone columns, is an elaborate image of the Egyptian sun god, backed with radiating sun and flanked by six large, golden snakes.

Inside is elegance: polished marble, exotic wood, gold and statuary. There are offices, a library, dining room, kitchen, Council Room, "Temple Room" and a large meeting room. This room is like a luxurious theater, rather elegantly furnished and decorated.

The ceiling is dark blue, with lights set into it to give the appearance of stars. These lights can even be made to "twinkle" like stars in the sky. There is a stage, well-equipped, and it is all very nicely done. But the thing that is most noticeable is the way the walls are decorated with serpents. There are all kinds; some very long and large. Many of the Scottish Rite degrees include the representation of serpents and I recognized them among those decorating the walls.

It was all most impressive and gave me a strange mixture of the sensations of being in a temple and in a tomb — something sacred but threatening. I saw busts of outstanding men of the Rite including two of Albert Pike, who is buried there in the wall.

## INTERVIEWED BY THE SUPREME COUNCIL

The first day was devoted to registration, briefings and interviews. We were called into one of the offices, one at a time, and interviewed by three members of the Supreme Council.

When my turn came I was ushered into the office and seated. The very first question I was asked was, "Of what religion are you?" Not long before this I would have answered with something like, "I believe the Ancient Mysteries, the 'Old Religion,' and I believe in reincarnation." However, without thinking at all about how to answer, I found myself saying, "I am a Christian."

Then, to my surprise and theirs, I asked of them, "Are you men born again?" The man in charge quickly stopped me by saying, "We're not here to talk about that — we are here to ask *you* questions."

After they sent me back out I sat down and thought about it. When the next man came out, I asked him, "Did they ask you if you are a Christian?" He said, "Yes, they did."

"What did you tell them?" I asked, and he replied, "I told them 'Hell no, and I never intend to be!'"

Then he said a strange thing to me, "They said I'm going higher," and he left through a different door, looking pleased.

## BECOMING A SOVEREIGN GRAND INSPECTOR GENERAL

The second day was the day of the actual initiation, held in the theater-like meeting room. Those of us who were receiving the degree were seated and the ceremony was "exemplified" (acted out in full costume) before us, in the same way that we had performed the lesser degrees of the Scottish Rite all those years. The parts in the exemplification were played by men of the 33rd Degree.

The representative candidate was dressed in black trousers, barefooted, bareheaded and draped in a long, black robe that reminded me of a very long, black raincoat. He had a black cabletow around his neck but was not hoodwinked. During the initiation he was led around the stage, conducted by two men with swords, as the degree was performed for us.

Instructions and signs were given. Upon the altar were four "holy books" (the Bible, the Koran, the Book of the Law and the Hindu Scriptures). At one point the "candidate" was told to kiss the book "of your religion" and, representing us all, he leaned forward and did so. I remembered the First Degree initiation, when I was told to kiss the Bible, and at that moment something came full cycle. It was the final such kiss to be a part of my life.

## WINE IN A HUMAN SKULL

When it was time for the final obligation we all stood and repeated the oath with the representative candidate, administered by the Sovereign Grand Inspector General. We then swore true allegiance to the Supreme Council of the 33rd Degree, above all other allegiances, and swore never to recognize any other brother as being a member of the Scottish Rite of Freemasonry unless he also recognizes the supreme authority of "this Supreme Council."

One of the Conductors then handed the "candidate" a human skull, upside down, with wine in it.

With all of us candidates repeating after him, he sealed the oath, "May this wine I now drink become a deadly poison to me, as the Hemlock juice drunk by Socrates, should I ever knowingly or willfully violate the same" (the oath).

He then drank the wine. A skeleton (one of the brothers dressed like one — he looked very convincing) then stepped out of the shadows and threw his arms around the "candidate." Then he (and we) continued the sealing of the obligation by saying, "And may these cold arms forever encircle me should I ever knowingly or willfully violate the same."

The Sovereign Grand Commander closed the meeting of the Supreme Council "with the Mystic Number," striking with his sword five, three, one and then two times. After the closing prayer, we all said "amen, amen, amen," and it was over.

## PROMINENT MEN TOOK PART

There were some extremely prominent men there that day, including a Scandinavian King, two former presidents of the United States, an internationally prominent evangelist, two other internationally prominent clergymen, and a very high official of the federal government, the one who actually presented me with the certificate of the 33rd Degree. Some made only brief appearances; others stayed much longer. However, they didn't do much mixing or socializing with us, except for those whom they already knew. Even though these celebrities weren't extremely "brotherly," it was still quite an experience for me just to be associated with them. It was easily the largest gathering of such prominent and influential men of which I have ever been a part.

The third day there was a banquet to celebrate our becoming "Grand Inspectors General, 33rd Degree." The banquet was a little anticlimactic, at least for me, and I was anxious to get it over with so I could return home. It was good to be a 33rd at last. But it wasn't as exciting or fulfilling as I had thought it would be during all those years in the Craft. I guess this was because of the profound changes going on down deep within me.

I returned home as soon as the 33rd Degree award and related social functions were finished, for it was time for my next appointment with the doctor. After he had examined my eyes he said that they were healing fine, that he felt good about the way they were looking, and as usual he spoke with me about the Lord. I told him that I planned to come to his church the next Sunday and that I had been reading the Bible.

Obviously pleased, he said, "Good. Keep studying, and your sight will soon be much better." By this time I knew what he meant — he was speaking of my spiritual sight.

## MAUNDY THURSDAY

In the Scottish Rite the Thursday before Easter, "Maundy Thursday," is an important day. On this day we always performed a special service of Communion in the local Scottish Rite Temple. At this time I was Wise Master in the Chapter of Rose Croix and it was my job to preside over the exemplification (dramatization) of the ceremony. I had done this many times and was known for my knowledge of the service and for "doing a good job" of putting it on.

## THE WORDS HAD MEANING NOW

On Thursday evening we gathered at our home Temple and dressed for the ceremony. It was always a most solemn occasion and seemed a little awesome, even to those of us who had done it many times.

Dressed in long, black, hooded robes, we marched in, single file, with only our faces partly showing, and took our seats.

There was something very tomb-like about the setting. The silence was broken only by the organ, playing mournfully in the background, and there was no light except for the little that came through the windows. After the opening prayer (from which the name of Jesus Christ was conspicuously excluded), I stood and opened the service.

As I had done so many times before, I said, "We meet this day to commemorate the death of our 'Most Wise and Perfect Master,' not as inspired or divine, for this is not for us to decide, but as at least the greatest of the apostles of mankind."

As I spoke these words that I had spoken so many times before I had a strange and powerful experience. It was as if I were standing apart, listening to myself as I spoke, and the words echoed deep within me, shouting their significance. They were the same words I had spoken so many times before, but had meaning for me now. They made me sick, literally ill, and I stopped.

The realization of what I had just said grew within me like the rising of a crescendo. *I had just called Jesus an "apostle of mankind" who was neither inspired nor divine!* There was a silent pause that seemed to last a very long time as I struggled with a sick smothering within.

When I was finally able, I continued with the service and we gathered around a large table across the room in marching order. The table was long, shaped like a cross, and covered with a red cloth which was decorated down the center with roses.

## A BLACK COMMUNION

Once we were assembled at the table, I elevated (lifted high) the plate of bread, took a piece, put my hand on the shoulder of the man in front of me, gave him the plate and said, "Take, eat, and give to the hungry."

This continued until all had partaken of the bread.

Then I lifted up the goblet of wine, took a sip, and said, "Take, drink, and give to the thirsty."

Again, this continued until all had partaken of the wine.

Then I took the bread, walked over to the first row of spectators and served it to the man previously chosen for the honor of representing the rest of the Lodge.

As I handed it to him I again said, "Take, eat, and give to the hungry."

In like manner I served the wine to him saying, "Take, drink, and give to the thirsty," and he sat down.

After this we took our places at the table shaped like a cross and sat down. The setting was dark, our long, sweeping robes were solid black, our faces nearly concealed in the hoods, and the mood was one of heavy gloom. The Christ-less prayers and the hymns we sang fit right in. The one word that would describe the entire event would be "black." It was, indeed, a Black Communion — a strange Black Mass.

## EXTINGUISHING THE CANDLE

There was a large Menorah (candlestick with seven candleholders) in the center of the room, with seven candles now burning.

Standing again, I said, "This is indeed a sad day, for we have lost our Master. We may never see him again. He is dead! Mourn, weep and cry, for he is gone."

Then I asked the officers to extinguish the candles in the large Menorah. One by one they rose, walked to the center of the room, extinguished a selected candle and left the room.

Finally, with only the center candle still burning, I arose, walked sadly to the Menorah and extinguished the last candle — the candle representing the life of Jesus, our "Most Wise and Perfect Master." We had dramatized and commemorated the snuffing out of the life of Jesus, **without once mentioning his name,** and the scene ended with the room in deep silent darkness. I walked out of the room, leaving only the darkness and the stillness of death.

Once again, the single word best to describe it would be "black."

All through the service I was shaking and sick. I have never felt so sad. I had stumbled over the words but, somehow, I made it to the completion of the ceremony and went back to the dressing room. I still didn't know much about praying but felt that I had been sustained by the Lord through it all.

## The Final Parting

Back in the dressing room we hung up our black, hooded robes, put our street clothes back on and prepared to leave. Less than two hours had passed since I arrived. But what had happened in that period of time had changed my life forever.

Still sick in my heart, I changed clothes without a word to anyone. The others asked me what was wrong. But I couldn't reply.

They reminded me that I had acted as Wise Master so many times before, that I was known for my smooth performance of it, and they asked what had gone wrong.

I was choking on the awful reality of what we had said and done, the way we had blasphemed the Lord, and the evil, black mockery we had made of His pure and selfless death. With weeping welling up within me, I could only shake my head in silence and walk out.

Mike was waiting for me at the door, expecting to get a ride home, and he asked, "What's the matter, Jim? Are you sick?"

Finally able to speak, I quietly replied, "No, Mike, I'm just sick of all *this*."

## "It Isn't Right"

I started down the wide steps in front of the large Scottish Rite Temple, realization and conviction growing within me, reached the bottom step and stopped. Turning around, I looked back at the huge, granite building and slowly studied the words, carved in the stone across the top of the entrance: "ANCIENT AND AC-CEPTED SCOTTISH RITE OF FREEMASONRY."

Something came clearly into focus in my understanding and I made a decision. This crisis point in my life, one which had required so many years for me to reach, passed in seconds. The truth was revealed and the choice was made — a choice that would be the difference between darkness and light, death and life, one that would last for eternity. Looking up at those words I had walked under so many times, words of which I had been so proud, I spoke to myself out loud. It was as if I were the only man in the world as I heard myself say, slowly and deliberately, "It *isn't* ancient, it *isn't* Scottish, it *isn't* free, and it *isn't right !*"

## INTO THE LIGHT

I turned away and walked into the parking lot, knowing that I would never return. As I walked into the deepening darkness of that springtime night, I was walking into the growing light of the living God. As the natural darkness closed around me, the supernatural light welled up within me. With every step I took, as the Temple receded behind me, I was more free.

"I will never return," I thought with each step. "I will never return, I will never return..."

The decision was made, the die was cast. From that night onward I would serve the true and living God, not the Great Architect of the Universe. I would exalt and learn of Him, not Osiris, Krishna or Demeter. I would seek and follow Jesus, not the will-o'-the-wisp of "hidden wisdom."

I was walking, after such a long time, out of the darkness and into the light.

### Footnote

[1]*This statement is an interesting contradiction with the Temple it adorns, as well as with the thousands of other such Masonic temples built around the World at a total cost of many billions of dollars.*

# Chapter II

# WALKING IN THE LIGHT

I tried to explain to Mike that Thursday night, and told him quietly but forcefully that I was *never* going to return to the Lodge. He looked at me for a few seconds, trying to understand, but unable to do so.

Then he said, "Alright, Jim, but what you need is a drink. Let's go get one."

"Alright, Mike," I replied, "but just one." As we started for the bar near where he lived, I said, "I don't think I'll have a drink, Mike. I think I'll just have a soda with you."

## A FRIEND LOVETH AT ALL TIMES

As we sat in the bar Mike continued to ask questions, trying to understand what was happening. I answered him as well as I could. He knew that I had dedicated my life to Masonry and how hard I had worked in it. He had been there with me for many years, working beside me when others were not willing to work. Since his first moment as a Masonic candidate, we had been together. I had urged him to join, had given him his petition, sponsored him and, as Senior Deacon, I was escorting him through the Blue Degrees when he threw Jubela across the Lodge Hall and established the "Honds-Off Policy."

We had worked together in the Scottish Rite Degrees so many times, working harder than all the rest. He had even taken time off

**111**

and gone with me when I received the K.C.C.H. If anyone on earth knew how truly I had loved and served Masonry, and how hard I had worked in and for it, it was Mike.

Now he was mystified, trying to understand why I was leaving it, but unable to do so.

The supernatural battle that had been going on within me was one of which Mike had not been a part. The truth of Scripture that had been lodged inside me from the doctor's witnessing and my Bible study was something in which he had not participated. He could not understand the things of the Spirit of God. At that point even I didn't fully understand it all. I just knew it was real—I just knew it was true.

But Mike was a friend — a real one — and even though he couldn't understand this outrageous thing I was doing, he was still sticking by me. Like the friend of Proverbs 17:17, he was going to love me "at all times," and was going to stick with me through adversity. Sadly, the others would not feel that way about it. Finally Mike said, "Jim, I don't understand why you are leaving the Lodge, but I hope you won't be angry with me if I *don't* leave."

I assured him that I *did* understand his position and that neither his staying nor anything else would ever cause me to stop being his friend.

## MAKING IT OFFICIAL

The next day I went to work. During my lunch period I wrote four letters of resignation: to the Blue Lodge, the Scottish Rite, the Eastern Star and the Shrine. I sealed, stamped, and dropped them into the mailbox in front of the office. I have never forgotten the "clang" of the mailbox lid when it fell shut. It seemed as though that sharp and sudden sound had severed something and set me free; I felt as if that "clang" sent a new life surging through me. However, that was not to be the end of Freemasonry in my life — not by any means. It was not going to be that easy.

## MY LAST MASONIC FUNERAL

The next day was my day off from work and I was at home when the phone rang. It was the Worshipful Master of the Blue Lodge and he said, "Jim, we are having the funeral for George (the Tiler[1] of the Lodge) this afternoon. Be at the Lodge Hall at 1 p.m. for the Lodge of Sorrows (the Masonic funeral is always begun and ended at the Lodge Hall).

Before I could reply, he hung up. I had only put my letters of resignation in the mailbox after noon the day before. Yet, somehow, they *already knew!* "How could they know *already?*" I wondered. It was obvious that they were not going to let me go so easily.

I had no intention of going to that funeral and it never occurred to me that they might come to get me. But that is exactly what they did. About an hour after the phone call, they drove up to the front of my house and the Worshipful Master came to the door.

He said, "Jim, I thought you would be at the Lodge of Sorrows; are you ready to go?"

I just looked at him for a moment or two and then said, "I'm not going."

## "JIM, YOU HAD BETTER GO"

"WHAT DO YOU MEAN, YOU ARE NOT GOING?" he burst out angrily. "OF COURSE YOU ARE GOING!" Then, more quietly, he said, "Come on, let's go."

I didn't move, and said, "I have just put in for a *demit.*"[2]

He wasn't at all surprised, but said, "Jim, you must be out of your mind! As long as you have served the Lodge, have served as Worshipful Master, and all the honors you have received, how can you do this?"

The tension was very great, and at that point Bonnie spoke up and said, "Jim, you had better go."

By this time I was beginning to wonder if they were planning to take me out and dispose of me, or perhaps keep me a prisoner until I "regained my sanity." But I said no more, kissed Bonnie goodbye and went out the door. At the car I stopped. I only had on trousers and a shirt. It is necessary in a Masonic funeral that participants wear a coat and tie. Without a word, the Master opened the trunk, took out a coat and tie and handed them to me. He had anticipated this also.

"Here," he said. "I know you think you won't have to take part in the funeral because you are not properly dressed but I brought these for you. Put them on."

I put them on, he ushered me into the car, and we drove away. At the funeral home there was a brief service conducted by the dead man's church. Although we took no part in it, I noticed how *very* similar it was to Masonic services. It could almost have been lifted right out of Masonic rituals. There was no mention of Jesus at all. The man was a Christian Scientist.

## MY LAST MASONIC PRAYER

We left the funeral home and followed the hearse to the cemetery. In the graveside service I was "Great Lights Bearer;" I had a wooden tray, supported by a strap around my neck, and on the tray were the Book of the Law (Old Testament Scriptures), Square and Compass, the "Great Lights" of Masonry.

The Master, who was Priest, stood at the head of the grave. I stood at the foot and the others lined up on either side. The Master did all the talking until time for the prayer. Then it was my turn. I had the "official" prayer card on the tray before me. I looked at that card, decided not to follow it, and then prayed my own prayer which I ended "in the name of Jesus Christ our Savior."

I had come a long way from that day when I had been made Chaplain in the Lodge of Perfection and didn't know how to pray; something else had come full cycle. The prayer was greatly offensive to the Master and the other Masons who were there, of course, but because of the setting not a word could be said to me about it.

## "ALAS, MY BROTHER."

We all had a sprig of Acacia which we dropped, in turn, into the grave and said, "Alas, my brother."

I dropped my sprig into the grave, said, "Alas, my brother," and it was as if I were looking down through the grave, into a dark eternity.

I said, "George, I wish you could have known Jesus as your personal Savior but, alas, my brother, it cannot be so. It is now too late."

## "I WILL BE GLAD TO HAVE YOU GONE"

We got back into the car and drove to the Lodge Hall where we completed the service by closing the Lodge of Sorrows. I started to leave when the Senior Warden came up to me and wanted to know what had happened to me to make me think of leaving the Lodge.

I told him as plainly as I could that I had been saved, I now belonged to the Lord Jesus Christ, and I could no longer belong to the Masonic Lodge, or any other lodge which denied Him as Lord.

He immediately became very angry and shouted, "I WILL BE GLAD TO HAVE YOU GONE!"

I then insisted that I go to the office of the Secretary and talk with him and was allowed to do so.

## ONCE A MASON, ALWAYS A MASON

The Secretary had just received my letter.

"Jim," he said, "I can hardly believe you would leave the Lodge after all these years and after the hard work you have done and the honors you have received. I just can't believe it." I knew that he could not understand, but tried to explain that I was now indwelt by the Holy Spirit and that He would be grieved if I went back into a Lodge Hall.

At least the Secretary was not hostile and, with that, I left. Of course, in the eyes of Masonry I would never leave — not really. The obligations (oaths) are considered unbreakable.

As a matter of fact, the "demit," the Masonic form for withdrawing from the Lodge, is looked upon by the Lodge only as a document which keeps you in good standing for the day when you will return. They do not look upon it as anything like a final resignation. From the Masonic point of view, the only way one can actually stop being a Mason is to die (and that, because of the general belief in reincarnation and the Masonic concept of Heaven, is not even the end of it in their eyes).

After I got back home I called Mike at work and told him all that had happened. He said that he wished he could have been at the service for the Tiler, for he had been a nice guy. Beyond that he made no reply. Mike was doing a lot of thinking.

## BEGINNING A NEW LIFE

Jesus was now in my heart and everything was changing. I was seeing things in a different light, things I had never before seen at all. The Spirit of God was living in my human spirit at long last. A truly new life had begun.

There was still so much to learn, so much clutter in my mind that needed to be cleared out and thrown away. But I was on my way. I was learning to walk in the light and the Light of the World was my constant companion and guide. It was wonderful.

Bonnie and I began attending the doctor's church regularly. After a lifetime outside of church, a lifetime filled with pagan religion and occult philosophy, it should have seemed strange to begin suddenly to attend church regularly. It should have been a cultural, emotional and spiritual shock for us — especially in *that* church (where the Gospel was plainly declared and Jesus exalted). But it seemed natural to be there. It was where we belonged.

## DRINKING IN A NEW LIFE

We also began to attend night classes at the Bible College associated with the church. It was a totally positive experience. From the very beginning everything we learned was a blessing — so positive, so "right" — that we wanted to learn more. What we were learning was not just interesting. It was like drinking in new life. We had, at last, found the real source of truth. We were taking in all that we could get.

## LEARNING TO LEAD SOMEONE TO THE LORD

After a few weeks of classes in the Bible college I had learned enough to realize that I really didn't know very much. Most importantly, I didn't know how to lead someone else to the Lord — that is, to help someone have the personal relationship with Him that I had found.

Except for the doctor's witnessing to me and the Scriptures he had shared, my being saved had been a thing entirely between the Lord and me. I wasn't even certain as to just how or when it had happened. I was learning that there are effective ways to witness, to approach people with the Good News, and that it is important to be able to show them the basis for it in the Bible.

But I also realized the importance of knowing how actually to lead someone to the Lord and I knew that I didn't know how to do it.

So I asked one of the teachers at the college, a man who had been a missionary to Cuba, to teach me.

He told me that there are many ways to approach it, taught me his method, and then gave me some tracts he had written. He advised me to memorize the verses of Scripture (such as John 1:12, John 3:3, John 3:16, Romans 3:23, Romans 6:23, Romans 5:8 and Romans 10:9, 10, 13) and the basic outlines of the tracts. I did just that and soon I was ready.

## The winning of mike

Vacation time was coming soon and I asked Mike if he could get his at the same time as mine. I told him that the house needed painting and, since we had done it together in the past, I hoped he could help me with the job again. He agreed, our vacations were arranged for the same period of time, and when the day arrived we went to work. We would work for about two hours, then stop for a coffee break at the kitchen table.

I had made plans to witness to Mike during the painting project and, at the first break, on the first day, I began.

"Mike, do you ever worry about what would happen if you should die?"

He said, "I worry about it sometimes but you and I decided to believe in reincarnation. Also, as a Catholic I was taught to believe in Purgatory, a place where I could spend time to pay for my sins."

I said, "Mike, I was wrong about reincarnation. The Bible says (in Hebrews 9:27) that 'it is appointed unto men once to die, but after this the judgment.' If reincarnation is true, the death of Jesus was for nothing because we would eventually save ourselves. And as for Purgatory, there is no Scripture for that idea, not even in Catholic Bibles."

I could tell that Mike didn't want to hear any more just then, so I let the subject drop; but I could also tell he was really thinking. He was very quiet and ordinarily he would have been doing a lot of laughing and joking.

## "I NAVE LED A VERY WICKED LIFE"

At the next break I asked Mike if he would like to go to Heaven when he died.

He said, "I have thought about it and, of course, I would; but I have led a very wicked life. I believe the Masonic Lodge has helped me, because I have a purpose now and things are much more regular. I don't know as much about the Bible as you do but if you want to talk about it I will listen."

So I said to him, "Mike, I am asking you the most important question of your life — your joy and peace for all eternity depend on your answer. Are you willing to receive the Lord Jesus Christ as your personal Savior?"

Without waiting for his answer, I went on. "You say that you have led a wicked life but if you are willing to confess your sins to Him and receive Him as Savior and Lord, all your sins will be forgiven and forgotten, washed away in His blood, and your life will have a new beginning. There is no other way to have all this; Jesus said, 'no man cometh to the Father but by me.' He also said, 'ye must be born again.'"

Mike just lowered his head and quietly said, "I don't know how to be born again."

I said, "Mike, would you be willing to try if I show you how?" With his head still down as if already in prayer, he quietly said, "Yes."

## IN MOMENTS IT WAS DONE

We got down on our knees, right there in the kitchen, and prayed. First I prayed for him and then I led him in a simple prayer, asking Jesus to forgive him, save him and to come into his heart to live. In moments it was done — a thing that would last for eternity.

Now Mike and I would no longer have to work and wonder, trying to be good enough to make it into "that Celestial Lodge above." Now we would be together, in the presence of our wonderful Savior, for all eternity. Mike was a child of God.

I told him to get up. He looked up at me, his eyes full of tears, and tried to thank me. But I told him only to thank the One who had died for him. Then I gave him some very simple instructions about reading the Bible and praying.

I asked him, "Mike, are you saved?" and he replied, very positively, "Yes, I *am!*"

We went back to work, were nearly finished when Bonnie came home, and we all had dinner together.

When I prayed over the food, Bonnie said, "Amen" and then Mike chimed in with a big "AMEN!" He was learning fast.

Later he asked me, "Jim do I now have t' give up smokin' me pipe?"

I said, "No, Mike — just let the Lord speak to you about it. But as you learn to stay close to Him, don't be surprised if He changes the way you feel about a lot of things."

I didn't ask Mike to leave the Lodge. But he immediately gave up all the degrees he was working in. He gave up the Shrine and seldom attended the Blue Lodge.

Because so many of the men kept asking him why he continued to speak to me after I had left the Lodge, he soon left the Scottish Rite altogether. For all practical purposes he was out of it all, although I had said nothing to him about it.

## SHUNNED BY THE BROTHERS

The change in our social life after I resigned from the Lodge was immediate and complete. Bonnie and I were cut off. For all those years we had been so busy with social functions and most of it was pleasant. Suddenly we were shunned by our friends. It was as if we had leprosy.

Not only had we been busy with parties, banquets and receptions associated with the Lodges, we had enjoyed so many good times in one anothers' homes. Never did I enjoy being a Mason more than at these informal parties in the homes. In our home we had entertained as many as 20 guests at a time—complete with music —and there was never a guest who left unhappy. We met so many friendly people at these parties that it was seldom we went anywhere in the city that we didn't see someone we knew.

Now, not a one of them would even speak to us when we chanced to meet, with the single exception of Mike. He stuck by us from the start and it was the hostility with which the rest treated us that hastened his decision about leaving the Lodge. I never had a better friend, nor a more stubborn one, than Mike.

Now, however, we were making new friends in the church and in the Bible College classes. The social functions that we were beginning to enjoy with our new friends were a lot healthier than the ones we had known before.

## PERSECUTION ON THE JOB BRINGS BLESSING

On my job, I was almost immediately changed to the night shift. There was no attempt to conceal the fact that it was because of my leaving the Lodge.

At first I was stung by it. But the Lord quickly showed me that it was a blessing. As was the case with Joseph of old, what was intended for evil, the Lord had used for good. Now I was able to enroll in the daytime program in the Bible College. Because the work wasn't so demanding on the job at night, I could do my studying at work and still do my job well.

## UNCLE IRVIN'S PARTING WORDS

My half-sister in Indianapolis called me one day to tell me that Uncle Irvin was in failing health and that she thought that I should see him. I returned to Indianapolis and the two of us drove out to his house.

Uncle Irvin did look ill, as if he might not live much longer.

I wanted to know that he would be with the Lord when he died, but I didn't get to speak with him about his salvation. He had already found out about my leaving the Lodge and was not at all open to hearing my reasons. He was already upset when I got there and went immediately to the attack.

Quickly becoming very angry, he shouted at me, "Don't you ever THINK? Don't you realize that Masonry is the SAME as JESUS CHRIST?"

I made no reply, for he expected none, nor would he listen to me. So, with this ultimate deception of the Masonic philosophy expressed in a few angry words ringing in our ears, we left. I never saw Uncle Irvin again.

In a matter of weeks he was dead.

## THE PAST IS PROLOGUE

I returned home, heavy in heart for Uncle Irvin, and went back to work. I had my job to do and my studies at the Bible College to pursue. There was so much to learn and I was hungry to learn it all.

Like my days in the Army in World War II, I was much older than the rest of the students. It didn't bother me at all. As a matter of fact, in some ways it was an advantage, for I had seen a lot of life and death that they hadn't seen.

There were many of them, for example, who were timid about speaking before a group. For me this was not a problem. My many years as a leader in the Lodge had provided rich experience in public speaking. When I went regularly to minister in one of the nursing homes, two or three of them would often go with me. They would help me with the music. I helped them to overcome the fear of public speaking. My Masonic years definitely paid off in this way.

## SO MANY MEN LIKE ME

There were many times when I would think about all those years I walked in darkness and wondered what I might have been able to do had I used all that time for the Lord. I felt that, somehow, it was not all wasted. As He promised in Romans 8:28, God could work it all together for good. He could convert those "wasted" years into something useful. If nothing else, those years in Masonry had equipped me to reach out to other Masons with the truth, the simple truth that can set them free.

"There are so many men like me out there," I thought, "so many Mikes, so many Uncle Irvins, deceived and being destroyed by a deadly deception. Some of them might listen to me."

## AT THE END OF A LONG NIGHT

Very early one morning, as a long night was giving way to the growing light of a bright new day, I stood on the pier, thinking. I looked back over all those years that seemed to have been wasted and tried to look into the years of my life that still lay ahead. I thought of how far I had traveled, searching for truth, seeking light, only to be led ever more deeply into the darkness by men who meant to do right. I thought of mother — looking so helpless as she sent me up the street and out of her life, with nothing to give me but her pitiful legacy of advice to try to be like Uncle Irvin.

I thought of all the men to whom I had passed on that deadly inheritance; and I thought of the longsuffering of God as He had pursued me through the years with His love.

"Maybe," I thought, "just maybe all this was preparation for serving Him. Maybe, with His Spirit to guide and strengthen me, I can lead some of those men out of the deadly deception of Masonry and into the truth and light of Jesus."

A ship was underway outbound, growing smaller as it followed the channel lights toward the open sea. Seagulls wheeled and circled overhead, squawking and seeking.

"Maybe that could be His plan," I thought "perhaps the Lord could use me to help them find their way. Maybe I can lead some of those empty, victimized men out of the pagan darkness of the Lodge and into the Light!"

With hope rising in my heart, with answers beginning to take shape in my understanding, and with a vision finding form in my spirit, I turned back toward the office. There was work to do.

------------------------------

"I am the Light of the World: He that followeth me shall not walk in darkness, but shall have the light of life."

**Jesus of Nazareth** John 8:12

### Footnotes

[1] *The Tiler is the officer in a Lodge responsible for keeping all "profane persons" (non-Masons) from entering the Lodge Hall. He is usually armed with a sword and guards the door during meetings.*

[2] *A "demit" is the Masonic form for withdrawal (becoming inactive) from the Lodge.*

# IN THE
# YEARS THAT
# FOLLOWED

Jim and Bonnie attended classes at the Bible college together and Jim continued his work with the Port Authority. Not long after leaving the Lodge, Jim suffered the first of two detached retinas. Laser surgery to restore his vision did so, but left him with sufficient visual handicap to eventually force his retirement after a bad fall on the job did additional, permanent damage to one of his eyes.

Two years after being born again, Mike began to have increasing pain and limitation in his back where he had been injured fighting the fire in New York so many years before. He also began to suffer a dramatic weight loss, and his once-powerful body became steadily weaker.

He was found to have cancer of the spine and died in the hospital where Jim had had his eye surgeries. During his last hospitalization, one of his old girlfriends came to see him. She asked Jim where the nearest Catholic church was, and said she would like to go there to light a candle for Mike.

Jim said, "He doesn't need a candle lit for him. Mike has Jesus in his heart now and his sins are all washed away."

Wearily, but gladly, Mike said, "Yes, that is true."

**123**

It was the last time Jim saw him alive. In less than two days Mike was dead.

Two years after retiring from the Port Authority, Jim graduated from Bible college. Since graduation he has preached, written many tracts and pamphlets and recorded many teaching tapes. He is dedicating the rest of his life to reaching other Masons with the simple good news of Jesus. He sends his teaching tapes, tracts and books all over the USA and to foreign countries. He carries on a steady correspondence with all who contact him for information. He and Bonnie still make their home in Florida, traveling with the message of truth and freedom as doors of ministry open.

Jim may be reached by writing to: *Rev. James D. Shaw, P.O. Box 884, Silver Springs, FL 32688*

— **Tom McKenney**

# A PERSONAL WORD FROM JIM

As this true story is closed, I would be greatly remiss if I did not make it clear that in my pre-Christian life I truly loved Freemasonry. I loved the men with whom I was associated in the Lodge and the men with whom I worked so hard in the degrees and bodies of the Scottish Rite. Most of all, I was so very sure that I was doing what was right and pleasing in the sight of the Great Architect of the Universe.

Never in all my years of dedicated service to Masonry did anyone in the Lodge witness to me about the love and saving grace of Jesus. The Lodge attended a church once each year as a group. Each time the pastor (who was himself a Mason) would introduce us to the congregation and then exalt the Craft, telling them about all our wonderful works. We usually left the church thinking of how wonderful we were and feeling sorry for all those in the church who were not Masons, participating in all our good deeds.

After having been witnessed to by my ophthalmologist for some time I read those simple, wonderful words of Jesus, "Verily, verily, I say unto you, he that believeth on me hath everlasting life." These words, so short and so sweet, went right through my heart. I looked in the Bible for more and I found blessed assurance everywhere I looked. Jesus the Christ, the Son of God, really loved me. That truth set me free. I received the One who loved me as a real Brother! He will do the same for you.

— Jim Shaw

# MASONIC DOCTRINE VERSUS CHRISTIAN DOCTRINE

The following is a brief comparison of the doctrines and practices of Freemasonry with the fundamental doctrines of the Christian faith and its foundational source, the Bible.

Masonic doctrines summarized here are, in every case, based upon the consensus of the most revered and widely accepted Masonic philosophers, writers and source-books. Any knowledgeable Mason will know at a glance that this is true. He has taken oaths to lie if necessary in order to conceal such things, and so will probably deny some things, and try to justify others. But the Masonic writers, and common practices in the Lodge, will verify it all.

Although most Masons have never read some of the sourcebooks cited, and have been deliberately deceived as to some of the facts in them, they could read them if they would. All these Masonic sourcebooks are in the libraries of most local Lodges and the libraries of all the Grand Lodges of the states. In addition, they can be purchased from Masonic publishing companies or in bookstores. But most Masons have never read them.

Many, many more similar references could be cited in addition to the ones included here but these will suffice. Capitalization and other means of emphasis are as the Masonic originals; nothing has been added or changed.

## 1. JESUS CHRIST

### a. MASONIC DOCTRINE

Jesus was just a man. He was one of the "exemplars," one of the great men of the

126

past, but not divine and certainly not the only means of redemption of lost mankind. He was on a level with other great men of the past like Aristotle, Plato, Pythagoras and Mohammed. His life and legend were no different from that of Krishna, the Hindu god. He is "the son of Joseph," not the Son of God.

(1) *"Nor can he (the Christian Mason) object if others see (in Jesus) only the Logos of Plato, and the Word or Uttered Thought or first Emanation of Light, or the Perfect Reason of the Great, Silent Supreme, Uncreated Deity, believed in and adored by all." (Albert Pike, "Morals and Dogma," 26th Degree, p. 524)*

(2) *"And the Divine Wise Intellect sent teachers unto men... Enoch, and Noah, and Abraham, and Moses the son of Imram, and the Prophets, and Pythagoras, and Plato, and Yesus the son of Joseph, the Lord, the Messiah, and his Apostles, and after these Mohammed the son of Abdulla, with his law, which is the law of Islam; and the disciples of truth followed the law of Islam." (Albert Pike, "Morals and Dogma," 25th Degree, p. 34)*

(3) *"In his private petitions a man may petition God or Jehovah, Allah or Buddha, Mohammed or Jesus; he may call upon the God of Israel or the First Great Cause. In the Masonic Lodge he hears petition to the Great Architect of the Universe, finding his own deity under that name. A hundred paths may wind upward around a mountain; at the top they meet." (Carl H. Claudy, "Introduction to Freemasonry," p. 38*

(4) *"It has been found that every act in the drama of the life of Jesus, and every quality assigned to Christ, is to be found in the life of Krishna" (Sun god of India) (J.D. Buck, "Mystic Masonry," pp.119, 138)*

(5) *"We meet this day to commemorate the death (of Jesus), not as inspired or divine, for this is not for us to decide," (Maundy Thursday Ritual, Chapter of Rose Croix)*

## b. CHRISTIAN DOCTRINE

Jesus Christ is divine, eternal and the second Person of the Godhead. When He was living on earth as a man, the only begotten Son of the Father, He was God incarnate, truly God and truly man. He was and is the only means of redemption of fallen mankind. Anyone who denies or rejects Him or His preeminent position as sole Redeemer also denies and separates himself from God the Father.

(1) *"In the beginning was the Word (Jesus) and the Word was with God, and the Word was God. The same was in the beginning with God. All things were made by Him; and without Him was not anything made that was made. In Him was life; and the life was the light of men." (John 1:1-4)*

(2) *"Jesus said unto them, 'Verily, verily I say unto you, before Abraham was, I am'." (John 8:58)*

(3) *"And now, O Father, glorify thou me with thine own self with the glory which I (Jesus) had with thee before the world was." (John 17:5)*

(4) *"Jesus saith unto him, "I am the way, the truth, and the life; no man cometh unto the Father, but by me'." (John 14:6)*

(5) *"Neither is there salvation in any other; for there is none other name (but Jesus) under*

Heaven given among men, whereby ye must be saved." (Acts 4:12)
(6) "He that hath the Son hath life; and he that hath not the Son of God hath not life." (I John 5:12)
(7) "Who is a liar but he that denieth that Jesus is the Christ? He is antichrist, that denieth the Father and the Son. Whosoever denieth the Son, the same hath not the Father." (I John 2:22, 23)
(8) "For there is one God, and one mediator between God and men, the man Christ Jesus." (I Tim 2:5)
(9) "I and my Father are one." (John 10:30)
(10) "... he that hath seen me hath seen the Father..." (John 14:9)

# 2. THE BIBLE

## a. MASONIC DOCTRINE

The Bible of the Christian is merely one of the "holy books" of man, no better than the Koran, the Hindu scriptures or the books of the Chinese and Greek philosophers. It is not to be taken literally, for its true meaning is esoteric (hidden from all but a small number of "enlightened," elite leaders); the literal, obvious meaning is only for the ignorant masses. It is right to remove references to Jesus in passages used in the ritual. Masonry, contrary to popular belief, is NOT based upon the Bible. Masonry is actually based on the Kabala (Cabala), a medieval book of magic and mysticism.

(1) "Masonically, the Book of the Law is that sacred book which is believed by the Mason of any particular religion to contain the revealed will of God... thus to the Christian Mason (it is) the Old and New Testament; to the Jew the Old Testament, to the Musselman (Muslim), the Koran; to the Brahman the Vedas; and to the parsee the Zendavesta." ("Masonry Defined," a compilation of the writings of Albert Pike and Albert Mackey, pp. 78, 79)

(2) "Masonry makes no profession of Christianity... but looks forward to the time when the labor of our ancient brethren shall be symbolized by the erection of a spiritual temple... in which there shall be but one altar and one worship; one common altar of Masonry on which the Veda, Shastra, Sade, Zend-Avesta, Koran and Holy Bible shall lie... and at whose shrine the Hindoo, the Persian, the Assyrian, the Chaldean, the Egyptian, the Chinese, the Mohammedan, the Jew and the Christian may kneel..." ("The Kentucky Monitor," Fellowcraft Degree, p. 95)

(3) "What is Truth to the philosopher, would not be truth, nor have the effect of truth, to the peasant. The religion of many must necessarily be more incorrect than that of the refined and reflective few... The truest religion would, in many points, not be comprehended by the ignorant... The doctrines of the Bible are often not clothed in the language of strict truth, but in that which was fittest to convey to a rude and ignorant people... the doctrine." (Albert Pike, "Morals and Dogma," 14th Degree, p. 224)

(4) "... the literal meaning (of the Bible) is for the vulgar only." (Albert Pike, "Digest of Morals

*and Dogma," p. 166)*

(5) *"To all this (error of stupidity) the absurd reading of the established Church, taking literally the figurative, allegorical, and mythical language of a collection of Oriental books of different ages, directly and inevitably led." (Albert Pike, "Morals and Dogma," 30th Degree, p. 818)*

(6) *"The Jews, the Chinese, the Turks, each reject either the New Testament, or the Old, or both, and yet we see no good reason why they should not be made Masons. In fact Blue Lodge Masonry has nothing whatever to do with the Bible. It is not founded on the Bible; if it was it would not be Masonry; it would be something else." ("Chase's Digest of Masonic Law," pp. 207-209)*

(7) *"Beautiful around stretches off every way the Universe, the Great Bible of God. Material nature is its Old Testament... and Human Nature is the New Testament from the Infinite God," (Albert Pike, "Morals and Dogma," 28th Degree, p. 715)*

(8) *"Masonry is a search after Light. That search leads us back, as you see, to the Kabalah. In that ancient and little understood (source-book) the Initiate will find the source of many doctrines; and (he) may in time come to understand the Hermetic philosophers, the Alchemists, all the Antipapal Thinkers of the Middle Ages, and Emanuel Swedenborg." (Albert Pike, "Morals and Dogma," 28th Degree, p. 741)*

(9) *"All truly dogmatic religions have issued from the Kabalah and return to it; everything scientific and grand in the religious dreams of the Illuminati, Jacob Boeheme, Sweden-borg, Saint Martin, and others is borrowed from the Kabalah: all Masonic associations owe to it their secrets and their symbols." (Albert Pike, "Morals and Dogma," 28th Degree, p. 744)*

(10) *The removal of the name of Jesus and references to Him in Bible verses used in the ritual are "slight but necessary modifications." (Albert Mackey, "Masonic Ritualist." p. 272)*

## b. CHRISTIAN DOCTRINE

The Bible is the *only* written revelation of, and from, the *only* true God. The Bible, as contained in the Old and New Testaments, is the Word of God, inspired and pre-served by Him, and is the only valid rule of faith and practice for His people, the church. No part shall be added to, or taken from the Bible as delivered to us in the Old and New Testaments.

(1) *"If they speak not according to this Word, it is because there is no light in them." (Isa.8:20)*

(2) *"All Scripture is given by inspiration of God." (II Tim. 3:16)*

(3) *"The Words of the Lord are pure words, as silver tried in a furnace of earth, purified seven times. Thou shalt keep them, O Lord, thou shalt preserve them from this generation forever." (Ps. 12:6, 7)*

(4) *"...whose hope is in the Lord his God, which made heaven, and earth, the sea, and all that therein is: which keepeth truth forever." (Ps. 146:5, 6)*

(5) *"Every word of God is pure: He is a shield unto them that put their trust in Him. Add thou*

*not unto His words, lest He reprove thee, and thou be found a liar." (Prov. 30:5, 6)*

*(6) "Heaven and earth shall pass away, but my words shall not pass away." (Matt. 24:35)*

*(7) "Being born again, not of corruptible seed, but of incorruptible, by the word of God, which liveth and abideth forever...But the word of the Lord endureth forever. And this is the word which by the gospel is preached unto you." (I Pet. 1:23, 25)*

*(8) "For we have not followed cunningly devised fables, when we declared unto you the power and coming of our Lord Jesus Christ, but were eyewitnesses of his majesty...Knowing this first, that no prophecy of the scripture is of any private interpretation. For the prophecy came not in old time by the will of man: but holy men of God spake as they were moved by the Holy Ghost." (II Peter 1:16-21)*

*(9) "Ye shall not add unto the word which I command you, neither shall ye diminish aught from it..." (Deut. 4:2)*

*(10) "...If any man shall add unto these things, God shall add unto him the plagues that are written in this book: And if any man shall take away from the words of the book of this prophecy, God shall take away his part out of the book of life..." (Rev. 22:18, 19)*

# 3. GOD

## a. MASONIC DOCTRINE

God is, basically, whatever we perceive Him to be; our idea or concept of God becomes our God. Usually referred to with the vague and general term, "Deity," the god of Masonry can be the one of our choosing, spoken of generically as "The Great Architect of the Universe." However, those who pursue the higher studies in Masonry learn that God is the force of nature, specifically the Sun with its life-giving powers. To the "advanced, enlightened ones," the adepts at the top, this nature worship is understood as the worship of the generative principles (i.e. the sex organs), particularly the phallus. Human Nature is also worshipped by some as "Deity," as are Knowledge and Reason. Since Masonry is a revival of the ancient pagan mystery religions, its god can also be said to be Nature, with its fertility (sex) gods and godesses representing the Sun and Moon (in Egypt, Osiris and Isis).

*(1) "...Since every man's conception of God must be proportioned to his mental cultivation, and intellectual powers, and moral excellence. God is, as man conceives Him, the reflected image of man himself." (Albert Pike, "Morals and Dogma," 14th Degree, p. 223)*

*(2) "...every religion and every conception of God is idolatrous, in so far as it is imperfect, and as it substitutes a feeble and temporary idea...of that Undiscoverable Being who can be known only in part, and who can therefore be honored, even by the most enlightened among His worshippers, only in proportion to their limited powers of understanding and imagining to themselves..." (Albert Pike, "Morals and Dogma," 25th Degree, p. 516)*

*(3) "The only personal God Freemasonry accepts is humanity in toto...Humanity therefore is the only personal God that there is." (J.D. Buck, "Mystic Masonry," p. 216)*

(4) "Phallus: a representation of the virile member (male sex organ) which was venerated as a religious symbol very universally...by the ancients. It was one of the modifications of Sun-worship, and was a symbol of the fecundating (impregnating) power of the luminaries. The Masonic point within a circle (important Masonic symbol) is undoubtedly of phallic origin." (Albert Mackey, "Symbolism of Freemasonry," p. 352)

(5) "These two divinities (the Sun and the Moon, Osiris and Isis, etc) were commonly symbolized by the generative parts of man and woman; to which in remote ages no idea of indecency was attached; the Phallus (penis) and Cteis (vagina), emblems of generation and production, and which, as such, appeared in the Mysteries (the ancient religions of which Masonry is a revival). The Indian Lingam was the union of both, as were the boat and mast and the point within the circle (important Masonic symbols)." (Albert Pike, "Morals and Dogma," 24th Degree, p. 401)

(6) "Masonry, successor to the Mysteries (the pagan religions of Isis, Osiris, Baal, Mythras, Tammuz, etc.), still follows the ancient manner of teaching." (Albert Pike, "Morals and Dogma," Fellowcraft Degree, p. 22)

(7) "Though Masonry is identical with the ancient Mysteries, it is so only in this qualified sense: that it presents but an imperfect image of their brilliancy, the ruins of their grandeur..." (Albert Pike, "Morals and Dogma," Fellowcraft Degree p. 23)

(8) "The Absolute is Reason. Reason IS, by means of Itself. It IS because IT IS...If God IS, HE IS by Reason." (Albert Pike, "Morals and Dogma," 28th Degree. p. 737)

(9) "This is the immutable law of Nature, the Eternal Will of the Justice which is God." (Albert Pike, "Morals and Dogma," 32nd Degree, p. 847)

# b. CHRISTIAN DOCTRINE

God is a Spirit, eternal, self-existent, unchanging, almighty and sovereign. There is one God who created all things, existing in three Persons: Father, Son and Holy Spirit. God the Father is revealed in His Son, Jesus Christ, and is perfect. He is holy, and requires holiness of His people.

(1) "In the beginning God created the heaven and the earth." (Gen. 1:1)

(2) "God is a Spirit: and they that worship Him must worship Him in spirit and truth." (John 4:4)

(3) "Hear, O Israel: the Lord our God is one Lord." (Deut. 6:4)

(4) "Before the mountains were brought forth, or even thou hadst formed the earth and the world, even from everlasting to everlasting, thou art God." (Ps. 90:2)

(5) "For I am the Lord, I change not;" (Mal. 3:6)

(6) "There is none other God but one...the Father, of whom are all things." (I Cor. 8: 4, 6)

(7) "But the Lord is the true God, he is the everlasting God, and an everlasting king." (Jer. 10:10)

(8) "Thy throne, O God, is forever and ever." (Ps. 45:6)

(9) "For there are three that bear record in Heaven, the Father, the Word (Jesus), and the Holy Ghost: and these three are one." (I John 5:7)

(10) "...Ye shall be holy: for I the Lord your God am holy." (Lev. 19:2)

(11) "God said unto Moses, 'I am that I am...'" (Ex. 3:14)

# 4. REDEMPTION

## a. MASONIC DOCTRINE

Redemption is a matter of self-improvement, morality, and good works, including obedience to the Mason's obligation and all higher Masonic authorities.

Faith in the atonement of Jesus has nothing to do with it; it is rather a matter of enlightenment, step by step, which comes with initiation into the Masonic degrees and their mysteries.

(1) *"By the lambskin the Mason is reminded of that purity of life and rectitude of conduct which are so essentially necessary to his gaining admission into the Celestial Lodge above, where the Supreme Architect of the Universe presides." (Albert Mackey, "Encyclopedia of Freemasonry," "Apron")*

(2) *"...and in Thy favor, may we be received into Thine everlasting kingdom, to enjoy, in union with the souls of our departed friends, the just reward of a pious and virtuous life. Amen. So Mote it Be." ("Texas Monitor," Masonic Burial Service, p. 10)*

(3) *"In Egypt, Greece and among other ancient nations, Freemasonry was one of the earliest agencies employed to effect improvement and enlightenment of man...and make them comprehend the true principles of morality, which initiate men into a new order of life." (Daniel Sickles, "Ahimon Rezon or Freemason's Guide," p 57)*

(4) *"The rite of induction signifies the end of a profane and vicious life, the palingenesis (new birth) of corrupt human nature, the death of vice and all bad passions and the introductions to the new life of purity and virtue." (Daniel Sickles, "Ahimon Rezon or Freemason's Guide," p. 54)*

(5) *These three degrees (1st, 2nd, 3rd) thus form a perfect and harmonious whole, nor can it be conceived that anything can be suggested more, which the soul of man requires" (Daniel Sickles, "Ahimon Rezon or Freemason's Guide," p. 196)*

(6) *"If we with suitable true devotion maintain our Masonic profession, our faith will become a beam of light and bring us to those blessed mansions where we shall be eternally happy with God, the Great Architect of the Universe." (Daniel Sickles, "Ahimon Rezon or Freemason's Guide," p. 79)*

(7) *"Acacian: a term signifying a Mason who by living in strict obedience to obligations and precepts of the fraternity is free from sin." (A. Mackey, "Lexicon of Freemasonry," p. 16)*

(8) *"When you shall have become imbued with the morality of Masonry...when you shall have learned to practice all the virtues which it inculcates; when they become familiar to you as your Household God; then will you be prepared to receive its lofty philosophical instruction, and to scale the heights upon whose summit Light and Truth sit enthroned. Step by step men must advance towards Perfection; and each Masonic Degree is meant to be one of those steps." (Albert Pike, "Morals and Dogma," 8th Degree, p. 136)*

(9) *"The dunces who led primitive Christianity astray, by submitting faith for science...have succeeded in shrouding in darknesss the ancient discoveries of the human mind; so that now we grope in the dark to find again the key..." (Albert Pike, "Morals and Dogma," 28th Degree, p. 732)*

*(10) "...salvation by faith and the vicarious atonement were not taught as now interpreted, by Jesus. nor are these doctrines taught in the esoteric scriptures. They are later and ignorant perversions of the original doctrines."(J.D.Buck. "Mystic Masonry." p. 57)*

## b. CHRISTIAN DOCTRINE

All have sinned and fallen short of the perfection God requires: none is righteous in his own virtue and our own righteousness is as filthy rags compared with the righteousness of God. However. Jesus. God's only begotten Son, lived a sinless life for us. and laid down His life a perfect sacrifice to make atonement for our sins.

By faith in Him and His provisions for us we can be made the righteousness of God and be born of the Spirit of God into everlasting life, becoming a part of the family of God. There is no other way to be reconciled to God and live in His presence forever. We cannot, by our own efforts, redeem or perfect ourselves.

*(1) "As it is written. There is none righteous. no. not one." (Rom. 3:10)*

*(2) "For all have sinned and come short of the glory of God:" (Rom. 3:23)*

*(3) "But we are all as an unclean thing. and all our righteousnesses are as filthy rags:" (Isa. 64:6)*

*(4) "For He hath made Him to be sin for us. who knew no sin: that we might be made the righteousness of God in Him." (II Cor. 5:21)*

*(5) "For ye (Christians) are all the children of God by faith in Christ Jesus." (Gal. 3:26)*

*(6) "For God so loved the world. that he gave his only begotten Son. that whosoever believeth in him should not perish. but have everlasting life." (John 3:16)*

*(7) "For by grace are ye saved through faith. and that not of yourselves: it is the gift of God: Not of works. lest any man should boast." (Eph. 2:8. 9)*

*(8) "Neither is there salvation in any other (than Jesus): for there is none other name under heaven. given among men. whereby we must be saved." (Acts. 4:12)*

*(9) "And this is the record. that God hath given to us eternal life. and this life is in his Son. He that hath the Son hath life: and he that hath not the Son of God hath not life." (I John 5:11. 12)*

# 5. SATAN

## a. MASONIC DOCTRINE

Satan, as an enemy of God and his Kingdom. as an evil power seeking to tempt. deceive and destroy. does not exist. Mankind has merely "supposed" this. The usual Christian perception of Satan is merely a distortion of the truth about Lucifer. the "Light Bearer." who is actually good and the instrument of liberty. but generally misunderstood and maligned.

*(1) "The true name of Satan. the Kabalists say. is that of Yahveh reversed: for Satan is not a black god...For the initates this is not a Person. but a Force. created for good. but which*

may serve for evil. It is the instrument of Liberty or Free Will. (Albert Pike, "Morals and Dogma," Master Mason / 3rd Degree. p 102)

(2) "Lucifer, the Light-Bearer! Strange and mysterious name to give to the Spirit of Darkness! Lucifer, the Son of the Morning! Is it he who bears the Light, and with all its splendors intolerable blinds feeble, sensual, or selfish Souls? Doubt it not!" (Albert Pike, "Morals and Dogma," 19th Degree, p. 321)

(3) "The conviction of all men that God is good led to a belief in a devil..." (Albert Pike, "Morals and Dogma," 19th Degree, p. 324)

(4) "All antiquity solved the enigma of the existence of evil by supposing the existence of a Principle of Evil, of demons, fallen angels...a Satan..." ("Kentucky Monitor," "The Spirit of Masonry," p xiv)

(5) "...there is no rebellious demon of Evil, or Principle of Darkness coexistent and in eternal controversy with God, or the Principal of Light..." (Albert Pike, "Morals and Dogma," 32nd Degree, p. 859)

## b. CHRISTIAN DOCTRINE

Satan is a proud, rebellious angel, created by God but fallen, the father of lies, accuser of the brethren, deceiver, tempter and ruler of the Kingdom of Darkness. He blinds the lost to the glorious light of the gospel, and seeks to be worshipped as he also works to steal, kill and destroy. He is the enemy we are to resist and the one whose works Jesus came to destroy.

(1) "How art thou fallen, O Lucifer, son of the morning! How art thou cut down to the ground, which did weaken the nations! For thou hast said in thine heart, I will ascend into heaven, I will exalt my throne above the stars of God: I will sit also upon the mount of the congregation, in the sides of the north: I will ascend above the heights of the clouds; I will be like the most High. Yet thou shalt be brought down to Hell..." (Isa. 14:12-15)

(2) "...Thou art the anointed cherub that covereth; and I have set thee so: thou wast upon the holy mountain of God; thou hast walked up and down in the midst of the stones of fire...Thine heart was lifted up because of thy beauty, thou hast corrupted thy wisdom by reason of thy brightness: I will cast thee to the ground..." (Ezek. 28:13-19)

(3) "Ye are of your father, the devil...he is a liar, and the father of it." (John 8:44)

(4) "And the great dragon was cast out, that old serpent, called the Devil, and Satan, which deceiveth the whole world: he was cast out into the earth, and his angels were cast out with him...the accuser of our brethren is cast down..." (Rev. 12:9, 10)

(5) "And Jesus being full of the Holy Ghost returned from Jordan, and was led by the Spirit into the wilderness, being forty days tempted of the devil..." (Lk. 4:1, 2)

(6) "And if Satan cast out Satan...how shall then his kingdom stand?" (Matt. 12:26)

(7) "Put on the whole armor of God, that ye may be able to stand against the wiles of the devil...For we wrestle...against the rulers of the darkness..." (Eph. 6:11, 12)

(8) "...the god of this world hath blinded the minds of them which believe not, lest the light of the glorious gospel of Christ...should shine unto them." (II Cor. 4:4)

(9) "The thief (Satan) cometh not, but for to steal, and to kill, and to destroy:" (John 10:10)

(10) "Resist the devil, and he will flee from you." (James 4:7)

(11) "For this purpose the Son of God was manifested, that he might destroy the works of the devil." (I John 3:8)

(12) "...Your adversary, the devil, as a roaring lion, walketh about, seeking whom he may devour:" (I Pet. 5:8)

# 6. SPIRITUAL LIGHT AND DARKNESS

## a. MASONIC DOCTRINE

All "profane" people (non-Masons), including godly, genuine Christians, are wretched, blind and lost in complete spiritual darkness. Only initiation into the degrees and mysteries of Masonry will bring them out of darkness and "into the light," cleansing them and imparting new life.

(1) "In Masonry, the darkness, which envelops the mind of the uninitiated (non-Mason) is removed by the effulgence of Masonic Light. Masons are appropriately called the 'Sons of Light'" ("Lightfoot's Manual of the Lodge," p. 175)

(2) "Freemasons are emphatically called 'Sons of Light'...while the profane or unitiated (non-Masons) who have not received this knowledge...are said to be in darkness." ("Masonic Dictionary," "Light," Consolidated Book Pub, 1963)

(3) Blindfolded ("hoodwinked") and kneeling, half naked and bound by a rope ("cabletow"), the candidate for initiation into the Blue Degrees is asked, by the Worshipful Master, "In your present, blind condition, what do you most desire?" His reply, according to the ritual, must be "Light" (1st Degree), "Further Light" (2nd Degree) and "More Light" (3rd Degree). (Verbal Masonic Ritual, 1st, 2nd, 3rd Degrees)

(4) "There he (the man to be initiated) stands, without our portals, on the threshold of his new Masonic life, in darkness, helplessness and ignorance. Having been wandering amid the errors, and covered over with the pollutions of the outer and profane world, he comes inquiringly to our doors, seeking the new birth, and asking a withdrawal of the veil..." (Albert Mackey, "Manual of the Lodge," p. 20)

(5) "Applied to Masonic symbolism, it (the darkness) is intended to remind the candidate of his ignorance, which Masonry is to enlighten; of his evil nature, which Masonry is to purify; of the world in whose obscurity he has been wandering and from which Masonry is to rescue him." (Albert Mackey, "Manual of the Lodge," p. 39)

## b. CHRISTIAN DOCTRINE

Jesus is the Light of the World; those who follow Him shall not be in darkness. He, and He alone, is the source of spiritual enlightenment. If we are "in Him" we are not in darkness, for in Him is no darkness at all. The life that He alone gives is the light of men.

(1) "I am the Light of the World: He that followeth me shall not walk in darkness, but shall have the light of life." (Jn. 8:12)

2) *"But ye are a chosen generation, a royal priesthood, an holy nation, a peculiar people; that ye should show forth the praises of him who hath called you out of darkness into his marvelous light." (I Pet. 2:9)*

(3) *"For ye were sometimes darkness, but now are ye light in the Lord:" (Eph. 5:8)*

(4) *"This then is the message which we have heard of him (Jesus), and declare unto you, that god is light, and in him is no darkness at all." (I Jn. 1:5)*

(5) *"In him (Jesus) was life; and the life was the light of men." (Jn. 1:4)*

# 7. PRAYER

## a. MASONIC DOCTRINE

Prayers are to be offered to "Deity," to "The Great Architect of the Universe" (GAOTU), and are to be "universal" in nature, so as not to offend anyone and so as to apply to everyone. Prayer is NEVER to be made "in Jesus' name," or "in Christ's name"; to do so would offend a Muslim, Hindu, Buddhist, etc. If a Worshipful Master allows prayers to be made in Jesus' name, his lodge can be closed and its charter revoked by the Grand Lodge of his state.

(1) *"All sectarian tenets must be carefully excluded from the (Masonic) system." (Morris, "Webb's Monitor," p. 285)*

(2) *"Prayer in Masonic lodges should be of a general character, containing nothing offensive to any class of conscientious brethren. (Ibid)*

(3) *"The religion then, of Masonry is pure Theism on which its different members engraft their own peculiar opinions; but they are not permitted to introduce them into the lodge..." (Albert Mackey, "Lexicon of Freemasonry," Religion)*

(4) *"Every important undertaking in Masonry is both begun and completed with prayer. The prayers given in the hand-books of the Blue Lodge are such as all Masons, whatever their religious faith, may unite in." (Morris's "Dictionary," Prayer)*

### NOTES:

(a) *It is true that in some local lodges, in small communities where all churches are Christian, prayers are made in Jesus' name. However, if this were to be reported to the Grand Lodge of that state they would be required to stop it immediately or have their charters revoked. Jack Harris, Worshipful Master of a Baltimore, Maryland lodge, was told just this. (Harris, Jack: Freemasonry: The Invisible Cult in Our Midst, Daniels Pub Co. 1983, pp ix, x, 121, 122)*

(b) *Harmon Taylor, former Grand Chaplain of the Grand Lodge of New York, says, "The only instruction I was given as New York State Grand Chaplain, and I was given it repeatedly, was not to end a prayer in Jesus' name. ("Attention Masons!", HRT Ministries, Box 12, Newtonville, NY 12128)*

(c) *It is a fact, known to every Mason who cares to know, that in all the prayers printed in his monitors, handbooks and other guides to rituals there is NOT ONE which closes in Jesus' name.*

## b. CHRISTIAN DOCTRINE

Prayer is to be made through the Father, in the name of (through) the Son, in the power of, and inspired by, the Holy Spirit. Only through the mediatorial office of Jesus can we approach the throne of God.

(1) "For there is one God, and one mediator between God and men, the man Christ Jesus." (I Tim. 2:5)

(2) "...whatsoever you shall ask of the Father in my (Jesus) name, he may give it to you." (Jn. 15:16)

(3) "Giving thanks always for all things unto God and the Father in the name of our Lord Jesus Christ." (Eph. 5:20)

(4) "And whatsoever ye do in word or deed, do all in the name of the Lord Jesus, giving thanks to God and the Father by him." (Col. 3:17)

# 8. TRUTHFULNESS

## a. MASONIC DOCTRINE

It is right to lie, if necessary, to protect the "secrets" of the Lodge, or to protect another Mason by concealing his wrongdoing. It can even be "right" to deliberately deceive sincere Masons seeking to learn the lessons and "secrets" of Masonry.

(1) "The Blue Degrees are but the portico (porch) of the Temple. Part of the symbols are displayed there to the initiate, but he is intentionally misled by false interpretations. It is not intended that he shall understand them; but it is intended that he shall imagine that he understands them... their true explication (explanation/understanding) is reserved for the Adepts, the Princes of Masonry." (Albert Pike, "Morals and Dogma," 30th Degree, p. 819)

(2) "Furthermore do I promise and swear that a Master Mason's secrets, given to me in charge as such, and I knowing them to be such, shall remain as secure and inviolable in my breast as in his own, when communicated to me, murder and treason excepted; and they left to my own election." (Master Mason's / 3rd Degree Oath of Obligation)

(3) "A companion Royal Arch Mason's secrets given to me in charge as such, and I knowing them to be such, shall remain as secure and inviolable in my breast as in his own, without exception." (Royal Arch Mason's Oath of Obligation)

(4) "You must conceal all the crimes of your brother Masons...and should you be summoned as a witness against a brother Mason be always sure to shield him... It may be perjury to do this, it is true, but you're keeping your obligations." (Ronayne, "Handbook of Masonry," p. 183)

(5) "If your wife, or child, or friend, should ask you anything about your initiation — as for instance, if your clothes were taken off, if you were blindfolded, if you had a rope around your neck, etc, you must conceal... hence of course, you must deliberately lie about it. It is part of your obligation..." (Ibid, p. 74)

### b. CHRISTIAN DOCTRINE

We must speak the truth at all times.

*(1) "Thou shalt not bear false witness against thy neighbor." (Ex. 20:16)*
*(2) "Ye shall not steal, neither deal falsely, neither lie one to another." (Lev. 19:11)*
*(3) "Lie not to one another." (Col. 3:9)*
*(4) "...all liars, shall have their part in the lake which burneth with fire and brimstone; which is the second death." (Rev. 21:8)*

# 9. SECRECY

## a. MASONIC DOCTRINE

Secrecy is the essence of Masonry, necessary for its very existence, and protected by blood oaths of mayhem and murder.

*(1) "Secrecy is indispensable in a Mason of whatever degree." (Albert Pike, "Morals and Dogma," 4th Degree, p. 109)*
*(2) "The secrecy of this institution is another and most important landmark...If divested of its secret character, it would lose its identity, and would cease to be Freemasonry... death of the Order would follow its legalized exposure. Freemasonry, as a secret association, has lived unchanged for centuries; as an open society it would not last for as many years." (Albert Mackey, "Textbook of Masonic Jurisprudence," 23rd Landmark, "Secrecy")*
*(3) "I...do hereby and hereon most solemnly and sincerely promise and swear that I will always hail, ever conceal and never reveal any of the arts, parts or points of the secret arts and mysteries of ancient Freemasonry which I have received, am about to receive, or may hereafter be instructed in..." (Oath of Obligation, Entered Apprentice/1st Degree, and included in all subsequent degrees, always on penalty of mayhem and violent death)*

## b. CHRISTIAN DOCTRINE

There are no secrets; the truth of God that sets men free is for all who will hear it, and we are to tell it to the world!

*(1) "I (Jesus) spake openly to the world; I ever taught in the synagogue, and in the temple...and in secret have I said nothing." (Jn. 18:20)*
*(2) "What I tell you in darkness, that speak ye in light; and what ye hear in the ear, that preach ye upon the housetops." (Matt. 10:27)*
*(3) "Go ye into all the world, and preach the gospel to every creature." (Mk. 16:15)*
*(4) "Provide things honest in the sight of all men." (Rom. 12:17)*

# 10. BLOOD OATHS

## a. MASONIC DOCTRINE

Blood Oaths on penalty of mayhem and violent death are administered at the end of initiation into all Masonic degrees, binding the initiate to protect the "secrets" of the degrees. These oaths of obligation (usually called just "obligation") are considered unbreakable, and are (collectively) the thing that makes a man a Mason. In this way, these oaths are the cornerstone of Masonry.

*(1) Question: "What makes you a Mason?" Answer: "My obligation." (question and answer from the Entered Apprentice/First Degree)*

*(2) "... binding myself under no less a penalty than that of having my throat cut from ear to ear, my tongue torn out by its roots, and with my body buried in the rough sands of the sea, a cable's length from the shore, where the tide ebbs and flows twice in twenty-four hours..." (from the oath of obligation, entered Apprentice/First Degree)*

*(3) "...binding myself under no less a penalty than that of having my left breast torn open, my heart plucked out, and given to the beasts of the field and fowls of the air as a prey..." (from the oath of obligation, Fellowcraft/Second Degree)*

*(4) "...binding myself under no less a penalty than that of having my body severed in twain, my bowels taken out and burned to ashes, the ashes scattered to the four winds of heaven..." (from the oath of obligation, Master Mason/Third Degree)*

*(5) "...In willful violation whereof may I incur the fearful penalty of having my eyeballs pierced to the center with a three-edged blade, my feet flayed and I be forced to walk the hot sands upon the sterile shores of the Red Sea until the flaming Sun shall strike me with a livid plague, and may Allah, the god of Arab, Moslem and Mohammedan, the god of our fathers, support me to the entire fulfillment of the same." (from the oath of obligation, Ancient Arabic Order of Nobles of the Mystic Shrine ["Shriners"])*

## b. CHRISTIAN DOCTRINE

A Christian is enjoined not to take oaths at all, especially oaths of mayhem and murder. It is particularly offensive to God for a Christian to take such an oath, swearing on the pagan Koran, calling upon Allah to sustain and make possible his faithfulness to the terrible oath, confessing Allah is "the god of our fathers." A Christian (or Jew) is not even to speak the name of a pagan god in a way that expresses respect or honor.

*(1) "Thou shalt not kill (do no murder)." (Ex. 20:13)*

*(2) "But I say unto you, swear not at all...but let your communications be, Yea, Yea; Nay, Nay; for whatsoever is more than these cometh of evil." (Matt. 5:34-37)*

*(3) "But above all things, my brethren, swear not, neither by heaven, neither by the earth, neither by any other oath: but let your yea be yea; and your nay, nay; lest ye fall into condemnation." (Jas. 5:12)*

*(4) "... and make no mention of the name of other gods, neither let it be heard out of thy mouth." (Ex. 23:13)*

# 11. SEEKING AND FINDING

## a. MASONIC DOCTRINE

Masonry is a never-ending search for "light," always promised but never quite realized.

(1) *"It is one of the most beautiful, but at the same time one of the most abstruse doctrines of the science of Masonic symbolism that the Mason is ever to be in search of truth, but is never to find it." (Albert Mackey, "Manual of the Lodge," p. 93; Daniel Sickles, "Ahimon Rezon or Freemason's Guide," p. 169)*

(2) *"You have reached the mountain peak of Masonic instruction, a peak covered with mist, which YOU in search for further light can penetrate only by your own efforts." (Lecture of the 32nd Degree, final earned degree, Scottish Rite)*

## b. CHRISTIAN DOCTRINE

If we sincerely seek truth (light) in Jesus, who declared Himself to be truth and light, we are promised that we will find it. Jesus is the beginning and the ending of our search. Coming unto Him we find life, meaning and understanding, for all that we need and desire, He provides. We are guaranteed, by God who cannot lie, that if we call upon Him we will not be disappointed or ashamed.

(1) *"And I say unto you...seek and ye shall find;" (Lk. 11:9)*

(2) *"... he that seeketh findeth;" (Lk. 11:10)*

(3) *"... him that cometh to me (Jesus) I will in no wise cast out." (Jn. 6:37)*

(4) *"For Christ is the end (fulfillment) of the law for righteousness to everyone that believeth." (Rom. 10:4)*

(5) *"... whosoever believeth on Him (Jesus) shall not be ashamed (or disappointed): (Rom. 10:11)*

# 12. EXCLUSIVENESS

## a. MASONIC DOCTRINE

The "light" of Freemasonry, its "secrets" and its pathway to "perfection" are only for the elite few initiated into its knowledge and wisdom. Excluded are women, Negros, the poor (who haven't the money with which to pay), the cripples, blind and deaf who can't perform the recognition signs (or see and hear them), and the feeble-minded who can't receive the teachings or be trusted to protect them. All such people, including the wives, the daughters and some of the sons of Masons, are considered "profane" (unclean, unworthy) and can never be anything else. No references are required here for it is common knowledge and all of the above confirms and establishes it.

## b. CHRISTIAN DOCTRINE

The life, knowledge, wisdom and freedom offered by God in Jesus are for "whosoever will"; anyone can come to Him and receive these priceless blessings, free, just by asking. Everyone who asks, sincerely, receives; none is turned away and none is disappointed or ashamed. God is not willing that anyone should perish, but wants all to come to Him and receive the life that He alone can give.

*(1) "The Lord is...not willing that any should perish but that all should come to repentence. (II Pet. 3:9)*

*(2) "Come unto me all ye that labour and are heavy laden, and I will give you rest. Take my yoke upon you and learn of me; for I am meek and lowly of heart: and ye shall find rest unto your souls." (Matt. 11:28, 29)*

*(3) "And let him that is athirst come. And whosoever will, let him take the water of life freely." (Rev. 22:17)*

# MASONIC SYMBOLISM

## 1. THE ULTIMATE DECEPTION

Masonry is, according to its own philosophers, a system of pure religion expressed in symbols, one which cannot be understood without a knowledge of the true meaning of them. This makes a proper understanding of those symbols terribly important. For the Christian Mason, accepting and guarding those symbols and their "secrets" with his physical life at stake, he must understand them to know that he is doing right.

For the many zealous Masons, trusting their obedience to their obligations to gain them entrance into that "Celestial Lodge Above," those for whom "the Lodge is a good enough religion," the correct understanding of these symbols is the key (they believe) to their eternal destiny. They are trusting in the teachings of the Lodge concerning these symbols with their eternal redemption, or damnation, at stake.

Herein lies the most terrible manifestation of Masonic morality, that philosophy of the elite, which makes whatever they do "right" because it is they (the elite) who do it. Having established and taught the sincere but deceived masses of Masons (the Blue Lodge Masons) that everything depends upon their proper understanding of the symbols of Masonry, they have then deliberately deceived them as to the true meaning of those symbols. Hear the arrogant words of Albert Pike, Supreme Pontiff of Universal Freemasonry, that preeminent Masonic authority: "The Blue Degrees are but the court or portico (porch) of the Temple. Part of the symbols are displayed there to the initiate, but he is intentionally mis-led by false interpretations. It is not intended that he shall understand them; but it is intended that he shall imagine that he understands them...their true explication (explanation and understanding) is reserved for the Adepts, the Princes of Masonry (those of the 32nd and 33rd Degrees)." (Morals and Dogma, page 819).

# 2. THE FOUNDATION OF MASONIC SYMBOLISM: PHALLIC WORSHIP

Since the true meaning of Masonic symbols (and, thus, the true meaning of Masonry itself) is to be known only by the Prince Adepts of Masonry, we must hear what they say concerning them. They (Albert Pike, Albert Mackey, J.D. Buck, Daniel Sickles and others) teach us that Masonry is but a revival of the Ancient Mysteries (the mystery religions of Babylon, Egypt, Persia, Rome and Greece).

These ancient religions had two meanings, or interpretations. One was the apparent (exoteric) meaning, known to the uninitiated, ignorant masses; the other (esoteric) meaning was the true meaning, entirely different, known only to a small, elite group, initiated into their secrets and secret rituals of worship. These mystery religions were forms of nature-worship, more specifically and most commonly the worship of the Sun as source and giver of life to the Earth. Since ancient times, this worship of the Sun (and of the Moon, stars and of nature in general) has been sexual in its outworkings and rituals. Since the Sun's rays, penetrating the Earth and bringing about new life, have been central to such worship, the phallus, the male "generative principle," has been worshipped as representing the Sun's rays. In this way, the phallus has been worshipped and the rituals climaxed with sexual union in the mystery religions of Isis and Osiris, Tammuz, Baal, etc. [1] In summary, then, since the Ancient Mysteries (especially those of Egypt) are in fact the "Old Religion" of which Freemasonry is a revival, the symbols of Masonry should be expected to be phallic in true meaning. This, in very fact, is the case. A thorough treatment of this unpleasant reality is beyond the scope of this brief summary; however, some examples, with references to the Masonic authorities, will suffice to illustrate this astonishing fact.

## a. THE SQUARE AND COMPASS

Blue Lodge Masons are taught that the Square is to remind them that they must be "square" in their dealings with all men, i.e. to be honest. The Compass, they are taught, is to teach them to "circumscribe their passions," i.e. to control their desires and to be temperate. The real meaning of these "great lights," however, is sexual. The Square represents the female (passive) generative principle, the earth, and the baser, sensual nature; and the Compass represents the male (active) generative principle, the sun/heavens, and the higher, spiritual nature. The Compass, arranged above the

Square, symbolizes the (male) Sun, impregnating the passive (female) Earth with its life-producing rays. The true meanings, then are two-fold: the earthly (human) representations are of the man and his phallus, and the woman with her receptive eteis (vagina). The cosmic meaning is that of the active Sun (deity, the Sun-god) from above, imparting life into the passive Earth, (deity, the earth/fertility goddess) below and producing new life. [2]

## b. THE LETTER "G"

The Blue Lodge Mason is taught that the "G" in the basic Masonic symbol represents God. Later on, he is told that it also represents "deity." Later still, he is told that it represents "geometry." In reality, this letter represents the "generative principle," the Sun-god and, thus, the worshipped phallus, the male "generative principle..." In its position (along with the Square and Compass) on the east wall over the chair (throne) of the Worshipful Master, it is the representation of the Sun, thus of the Sun-god, Osiris. Its earthly meaning, then, is of the sacred phallus; its cosmic meaning is of the Sun, worshipped since antiquity by pagans while facing the East. (See c, below).

## c. THE "G" AND THE "YOD"

The English letter "G" in Masonic symbolism is inseparable from, and identical with, the Hebrew letter "YOD." This "YOD" is the symbol on the Scottish Rite ring. "YOD" represents deity in general (its cosmic meaning), and the worshipped phallus in particular (its earthly meaning). Albert Pike wrote that the "G" displayed in English speaking lodges is merely a corruption of the "YOD" (with which it should be replaced), and that "the mysterious YOD of the Kabalah" is the "image of the Kabalistic Phallus."[3] The "Kabalah" he refers to here is a medieval book of the occult, a highly mystical and magical interpretation of the Bible,[4] and important sourcebook for sorcerers and magicians.[5]

## d. THE POINT WITHIN A CIRCLE

The Masons of the Blue Lodge are taught that the Point within a Circle represents the individual Mason (the Point), contained and restricted by the boundary line of his duty (the Circle). Its real meaning, however, is that of the phallus, positioned within the female generative principle (sex organ) in sexual union, the climactic act of Sun-god worship.[6]

Dr. Albert Mackey, already quoted herein, also writes in his classic work "Symbolism of Freemasonry," page 352, "Phallus, a representation of the virile member, which was venerated as a religious symbol... It was one of the modifications of sun worship, and was a symbol of the fecundating power of that luminary. The Masonic point within a circle is undoubtedly of phallic origin."

The cosmic meaning of this symbol is that of the Sun, surrounded by the Universe; on the following page (353) he writes, "Point within a circle. It is derived from Sun-worship, and is in reality of phallic origin. In his "Manual of the Lodge," page 156, Mackey writes, "The point within a circle is an interesting and important symbol in Freemasonry, but it has been debased in the interpretation of it in the modern lectures and the sooner that interpretation is forgotten by the Masonic student, the better it will be. The symbol is really a beautiful but somewhat abstruse allusion to the old Sun-worship, and introduces us for for the first time to that modification of it, known among the ancients as the worship of the phallus."

## e. THE VERTICAL LINES

The two vertical lines touching the sides of the circle are represented to the Blue Lodge Mason as "the Holy Saints John." By this is meant John the Baptist and John the Apostle. In reality, the two vertical lines represent the Summer and Winter Solstices, the shortest and longest nights of the year, respectively. These nights are, and have been since antiquity, important periods for pagan worship.

Concerning these two lines, Albert Mackey has written ("Symbolism of Freemasonry," page 352), "The lines touching the circle in the symbol of the point within a circle are said to represent St. John the Baptist and St. John the Evangelist, but they really refer to the solstitial points, Cancer and Capricorn, in the Zodiac."

## f. THE BIBLE

The Bible, only one of the "Three Great Lights" of Masonry (along with the Square and Compass), is represented to Blue Lodge Masons as symbolizing truth. In reality, the Bible may be replaced with the Koran, the Book of the Law, the Hindu scriptures or any other "holy book," depending on the preferences of the men in the Lodge. In most American Lodges, the members are told that all the Masonic system and its rituals are "based on the Bible." Such, however, is not the case. In Chase's "Digest of Masonic Law," pages 207-209, it is clearly written that "Masonry has nothing whatever to do with the Bible," and that "it is not founded upon the Bible, for if it were it would not be Masonry, it would be something else."

Albert Pike, in writing on the subject of Masonry's source-book said, "Masonry is a search after light. That search leads us directly back, as you see, to the Kabalah." (Morals and Dogma, page 741). The Kabalah, then, seems to be the actual sourcebook of Masonry and the Bible merely (as it is spoken of in the ritual) a piece of the "furniture" of the Lodge.

NOTE: For more information concerning Masonic symbols and their true meanings, see McQuaig, C.F., "The Masonic Report," Answer Books and Tapes, Norcross, GA 1976; Storms, E.M., "Should a Christian Be a Mason?," New Puritan Library, Fletcher, NC 1980; and Mackey, Albert G., "Symbolism of Freemasonry," Charles T Powner Co, Chicago 1975.

## Footnotes

[1] *"Phallus: a representation of the virile member (male sex organ) which was venerated as a religious symbol very universally... by the ancients. It was one of the modifications of Sun-worship, and was a symbol of the fecundating (impregnating) power of that luminary. The Masonic point within a circle is undoubtedly of phallic origin." (Mackey, Albert G., "Symbolism of Freemasonry," pg. 352)*

[2]*Pike, Albert, "Morals and Dogma," pgs. 11, 839, 850, 851.*

[3]*Pike, Albert, "Morals and Dogma," pgs. 5, 757, 758, 771, 772.*

[4]*"Cabala (Kabalah) is a medieval and modern system of theosophy, mysticism, and thaumatology (magic), "Webster's New Collegiate Dictionary, " pg. 53.*

[5]*Baskin, Wade, "The Sorcerer's Handbook," New York, Philosophical Library, 1974.*

[6]*"These two divinities... were commonly symbolized by the generative parts of man and woman... the Phallus and Cteis (vagina), emblems of generation and production, and which, as such, appeared in the Mysteries. The Indian Lingam was the union of both, as were the Boat and Mast, and the Point within the Circle... Pike, Albert, "Morals and Dogma," pg. 401.*

# MASONIC MORALITY

## 1. UNDERLYING ATTITUDES AND ASSUMPTIONS

There is, underlying all Masonic thinking and writing, an attitude and spirit of elitism which says, "Masonry is not for everyone, just for the select few." At the same time Masonry teaches it is the only true religion and that all other religions are but corrupted and perveted forms of Masonry. This is both elitist and contradictory, in that it leaves no hope for the non-elite to find the "true religion." Freemasonry proudly proclaims it makes good men better; but this makes no provision for bad men to become good.

### a. NO ROOM IN THE LODGE FOR THE BLIND, CRIPPLED, POOR, ETC.

It is significant, I think, that those whom Masonry rejects and excludes are the very ones Jesus sought out to accept and minister to.

The Lodge excludes and rejects the blind, for they cannot see to engage in the signs and due-guards; it rejects the crippled and maimed, for they cannot assume the body positions necessary for the signs and due-guards. The deaf are excluded because they cannot hear the "secret" words. The poor are excluded, for they cannot pay the fees and dues. The feeble-minded are rejected because they cannot learn and function in the Lodge. The emotionally ill are rejected because they cannot be trusted with the "secrets." Negroes and women are excluded simply because they are considered unsuitable.

Jesus, on the other hand, proclaims that His gift of redemption is for "whosoever will," and that all may "take the water of life freely" (Rev. 22:17). He especially reached out to the blind, the crippled, the feeble-minded and mentally ill, the poor and the unwanted — the very ones Masonry excludes and rejects.

## b. EVEN WITHIN THE LODGE THE ELITE SPIRIT RULES.

Even within Masonry the spirit of elitism, the principle of the superiority of the "chosen few," prevails. Those Blue Lodge Masons who lack the money cannot pursue the higher degrees and the Shrine. And, even for those who can afford the higher degrees and the Shrine, there are offices and positions closed to some who haven't the wealth, nice home or social position required.

## c. IT CAN BE "RIGHT" IN MASONIC MORALITY TO DECEIVE SINCERE MASONS.

The deadly danger of this elitist attitude ( in any organization or society) is that whatever the elite leadership decides is "right" is then right, regardless of external moral considerations. A significant case in point is the fact that the "ordinary" Masons of the Blue Lodge are deliberately deceived by the Masonic philosophers and writers of doctrine into believing they understand the meaning of Masonic symbols and rituals when they do not.

The masses of "ordinary" (Blue Lodge) Masons who pay the dues and work faithfully to make the entire system possible are deliberately deceived as to the true nature of what they are saying and doing. But this deliberate deception becomes "right" in Masonic morality, simply because the elite leadership decides that it is right. For documentation of this profound deception, see Appendix B, "Masonic Symbolism."

# 2. SPECIFIC EXAMPLES OF MASONIC MORALITY

So much of the morality expressed in Masonic teachings, particularly the oaths of obligation, sound good on the surface but do not stand up under casual scrutiny. Most Masons really believe they are binding themselves to moral standards of behavior. But this is because they have never really thought about what they have said. Their basic assumption that it is all "good" closes their eyes to the reality. Although volumes could be written concerning the flawed morality of Masonry, for the purposes of this brief summary a few examples will suffice. The following are selected examples of the moral standards of Masonry, compared with teachings of the Bible.

## a. FORNICATION AND ADULTERY

The Master Mason swears not to "violate the chastity" of the mother, wife, sister or daughter of another Master Mason, "knowing her to be such." This may sound good superficially, but it permits intercourse with anyone else's mother, wife, sister or daughter (even Masons of the First and Second Degrees), and permits intercourse with those of a Master Mason as long as one isn't aware of their Masonic relationship. It could even permit such illicit intercourse with female relatives of a Master Mason, knowingly, if they are not chaste and, therefore, have no chastity to be violated. The

Bible, on the other hand, is very clear concerning the matter. We are told to flee forni-
cation, and are forbidden to commit adultery (Ex. 20:14; Acts 15:20; I Cor. 6:18; et al).

## b. CHEATING, WRONGING, DEFRAUDING

The Master Mason swears not to "cheat, wrong or defraud" another Master Mason
or a Lodge of Master Masons, "I knowing them to be such." This may seem like lofty
morals to the casual observer, but it will not bear scrutiny. This promise permits the
cheating, wronging or defrauding of anyone not a Master Mason, or an organization
other than a Lodge of Master Masons, and even they may be cheated, wronged or
defrauded if the Mason doing it doesn't realize who or what they are.

The Bible is likewise very clear concerning this class of behavior, stating plainly
that we must not cheat, wrong or defraud anyone at any time (Ex. 20:15; Lev. 19:13,
35; Prov. 11:1; Eph. 4:28; et al).

## c. LYING AND PERJURING

The Mason swears to keep the secrets of another Mason, protecting him even if it
requires withholding evidence of a crime. In some degrees treason and murder are excepted; in other, higher degrees, there are no exceptions to this promise to cover up
the truth. The obligations, if the Masonic teachings are believed, may require a Mason
to give false testimony, perjure himself or (in the case of a judge) render a false verdict
in order to protect another Mason. Again, the Bible is quite clear in teaching that we
must never lie or bear false witness, and states that liars will have their part in the Lake
of Fire (Ex. 20:16; Prov. 19:5, 9; Eph. 4:15; Rev. 21:8; et al).

## d. HELPING OTHERS

The Master Mason swears to assist widows, orphans and others in need of help,
so long as it is not inconvenient or sacrificial for him to do so ("so far as...my abilities
permit without material injury to myself"). He also swears to go to the aid of another
Master Mason who gives the "Grand Hailing Sign of Distress," that most extreme call
for help, given only when life is threatened. However, he agrees to help that distressed
brother Master Mason only if he can do it without unduly risking his own life ("only
if there is a greater probability of saving the other's life than of losing my own"). Given
the wrong circumstances here, the Master Mason would apparently allow the other
Master Mason to die, to say nothing of one in peril who is not a Master Mason. The
most casual student of the Bible and its teachings knows that it teaches us to give to
those in need, whether or not it is easy, and that we are to consider others' needs,
comfort, lives, etc. more important than our own (Prov. 3:27; Matt. 25:31-46; John
15:12, 13; Jas. 2:15, 16; et al).

NOTE: For a more thorough study of Masonic morality and its flaws, see McQuaig,
C.F., "The Masonic Report," Answer Books and Tapes, Norcross, GA, 1976.

# CHE LEGEND OF HIRAM ABIFF
## (CHE EGYPCIAN CONNECCION)

The heart of Freemasonry is the Blue Lodge with its three degrees. The climactic degree (and the final one for most Masons) in the Blue Lodge is the Third, or Master Mason Degree. The heart of the Master Mason Degree, the thing that gives it both meaning and substance, is without any doubt the reenactment of the Legend of Hiram Abiff. It is this central figure in the legend, this Hiram "The Widow's Son," the "Tyrian Architect," this "First Grand Master" who is impersonated by every man who is initiated as a Master Mason. It is Hiram who is at the very heart of the foundation of all of Masonry. His true identity and nature become, then, matters of extreme significance. Just who — and what — was this man, Hiram Abiff?

## 1. THE MASONIC TRADITION

According to the Masonic legend, Hiram Abiff was a man of Tyre, the son of a widow, and the chief architect of the Temple built by King Solomon. He was the central character in the building of the Temple and one of three leading characters along with King Solomon and Hiram, King of Tyre. Hiram Abiff, Masonry teaches, was the only one on Earth who knew the "secrets of a Master Mason," including the most important secret of all, the "Grand Masonic Word," the name of God (the "ineffable name"). Since, in occult lore, knowing the name of a spirit is a key to having its power, there was very great power in knowing this word. Knowing the other "secrets of a Master Mason" would enable the masons/workmen working on the Temple project to go out on their own, working as Master Masons and earning "Master Mason's wages."

This Hiram had promised to reveal the "secrets of a Master Mason," including the name of God ("Grand Masonic Word"), upon completion of the Temple, and to make the workmen Master Masons, able then to go out on their own as masters (they were, as yet, only "fellowcraft" Masons). One day Hiram went, as was his custom, into the unfinished Holy of Holies at noon ("High Twelve") to worship and to draw up the work plans (on his "trestleboard") for the workmen to follow the next day. The workmen were outside the Temple for their lunch break ("...the craft were called from labor to refreshment...").

As Hiram was leaving the Temple he was accosted by three "ruffians," in succession, who demanded that they be given the secrets immediately (without waiting for the Temple to be completed). He was handled roughly by the first ruffian (Jubela), but escaped. Accosted and handled roughly by the second ruffian (Jubelo), he again refused to divulge the secrets and again escaped. The third ruffian (Jubelum) then accosted him and, when Hiram again refused to divulge the secrets, killed him with a blow to the forehead with a setting maul. The body was hastily concealed under some rubbish in the Temple until midnight ("low twelve") when it was taken out to the brow of a hill and buried. The grave was marked by a branch of Acacia (an evergreen tree common in the Middle East), and the three ruffians attempted to escape the country. Denied passage on a ship out of the country, they retreated into the hills to hide. Meanwhile, back at the Temple, it was noticed that Hiram was missing and King Solomon was notified. Solomon immediately ordered a search in and about the Temple with no success. At this point 12 "fellowcrafts" reported to the King that they and three others (the three "ruffians") had conspired to extort the secrets of Hiram Abiff but they had repented and refused to go through with the murderous plan. They reported that it was those other three who had murdered Grand Master Hiram and King Solomon then sent them out in groups of three to search in all directions.

After questioning the sea captain who had refused the murderers passage, three of the searchers then followed the murderers' path and discovered the grave with its Acacia at the head. Digging down and recognizing the body, they reported back to Solomon. Solomon sent them back to locate the grave, positively identify the body as Hiram and to attempt to raise it from the grave with the grip of an Entered Apprentice. They relocated the grave but were unable to raise the body because decomposition had caused the flesh to leave the bone.

Reporting back to Solomon, they were told to return to the grave and attempt to raise the body with the grip of a Fellowcraft. When this failed because the skin slipped away, they reported back to Solomon who, himself, went to the grave and raised the body up with the grip of a Master Mason, the "Strong Grip of a Lions Paw." Hiram was not only brought up out of the grave, but restored to life. The first word he spoke was the replacement for the "Grand Masonic Word" lost at his death and that word is the one passed down to Master Masons to this day.[1] This, then, is the Masonic legend of Hiram Abiff, and most Blue Lodge Masons believe that it is a factual, scriptural and historical account. It is generally believed, in spite of the fact that the Masonic authorities and writers of doctrine agree that it is not only a myth, unsupported by facts, but acknowledge that it is but a retelling of the legend of Isis and Osiris.

## 2. THE BIBLE RECORD

Does the Bible record such a person as Hiram Abiff? Definitely not, although part of his identity is taken from the Bible. The Scriptures record two men named Hiram concerning the building of the Temple by King Solomon; one is Hiram, King of Tyre, who was supportive of Solomon and who provided materials and workmen for the project. The other Hiram, called "a widow's son of the tribe of Naphtali," was a worker in brass, not the architect of the entire Temple. He made the brass pillars, the brass sea with its 12 oxen to support it, 10 bases of brass with brass bowls, and all the brass lavers, shovels and basins. The Scriptures record that this Hiram, the widow's son, completed all the work that he had come to do on the Temple. Presumably, he then returned to his home in Tyre, safe and sound (there is no indication in the Bible of anything to the contrary).[2] Concerning the Masonic claim that Hiram, the widow's son, was chief architect of the Temple, the Bible is clear in establishing that he was no such thing. The Bible reveals that God, Himself, was the designer and architect of the Temple, that He gave the plans in minute detail to David and that David gave them to Solomon,[3] along with most of the materials. To claim that anyone but God was the Chief Architect of the Temple is unfounded and, I believe, blasphemous.

## 3. THE EGYPTIAN CONNECTION

It is the consensus of opinion among Masonic authorities, philosophers and writers of doctrine that the legend of Hiram Abiff is merely the Masonic version of a much older legend, that of Isis and Osiris, basis of the Egyptian Mysteries. The following is a brief summary of that legend, and a comparison with the Masonic legend of Hiram Abiff. This comparison is supported, beyond doubt, by the conclusions of the Masonic authorities.

### a. THE LEGEND OF ISIS AND OSIRIS

Osiris, both King of the Egyptians and their god, went on a journey to bless neighboring nations with his knowledge of arts and sciences. His jealous brother, Typhon (god of Winter) conspired to murder him, steal his kingdom and did so. Isis, sister and wife of Osiris and his queen (as well as Egypt's Moon- goddess) set out on a search for the body, making inquiries of all she met.

After certain adventures, she found the body with an Acacia tree at the head of the coffin. Returning home, she secretly buried the body, intending to give it a proper burial as soon as arrangements were made. Typhon, by treachery, stole the body, cut it up into 14 pieces and hid them in as many places. Isis then made a second search and located all the pieces but one; the one missing and lost part was the phallus.

She made a substitute phallus, consecrated it, and it became a sacred substitute, an object of worship.

This, in extremely abbreviated form, is the Egyptian legend of Isis and Osiris. It is, without doubt, the basis for the Masonic legend of Hiram Abiff. To support this "Egyptian connection," let's consider two things: a brief comparison of key elements in both stories and the conclusions of the Masonic authorities in Masonic source-writings.

## b. A BRIEF COMPARISON OF THE LEGENDS OF HIRAM ABIFF AND OSIRIS

The fundamental similarity between the two stories may be seen in many respects; the following are some of the most important:

*(1) Both men went to foreign lands to share their knowledge of arts and sciences.*

*(2) In both legends there is a precious thing possessed: Hiram has the secret word; Osiris has the kingdom.*

*(3) In both legends there is a wicked conspiracy by evil men to seize the precious thing.*

*(4) In both legends there is a struggle and a murder of the virtuous leader.*

*(5) Both are murdered by their brothers (Osiris by Typhon; Hiram by Jubelum, his brother Mason).*

*(6) Both bodies are buried hastily, with the intention of a later, deliberate burial.*

*(7) Locations of the bodies are both marked by Acacia at the head.*

*(8) In both legends there are two separate searches for the bodies.*

*(9) In both legends there is a loss of something precious: in Hiram's death the secret word is lost; in Osiris' death the phallus is lost.*

*(10) In both there is a substitution for the precious thing that has been lost; concerning Hiram it is the substitute for the secret word; concerning Osiris it is the substitute phallus, made by Isis.*

## c. CONCLUSIONS OF THE MASONIC AUTHORITIES

A few statements from the most authoritative Masonic writers will suffice to express the doctrinal consensus:

*(1) "The legend and traditions of Hiram Abiff form the consummation of the connecting link between Freemasonry and the Ancient Mysteries." (Pierson, "Traditions of Freemasonry," page 159)*

*(2) "We readily recognize in Hiram Abiff the Osiris of the Egyptians..." (Pierson, page 240)*

*(3) "Osiris and the Tyrian Architect (Hiram Abiff) are one and the same." (Sickles, Daniel, "Freemason's Guide," page 236)*

*(4) "That part of the rite (Master Mason initiation) which is connected with the legend of the Tyrian Artist (Hiram Abiff)...should be studied as a myth and not as a fact...outside of*

*Masonic tradition there is no proof that an event such as is related in connection with the "Temple Builder" ever transpired and, besides, the ceremony is older by more than a thousand years than the age of Solomon... It is thoroughly Egyptian." (Sickles, Daniel, "The Ahiman Rezon," page 195)*

*(5) It (the Legend of Hiram Abiff) is thoroughly Egyptian, and is closely allied to the Supreme Rite (highest degree) of the Isianic Mysteries (Mystery religion of Isis and Osiris)." (Mackey, Albert, "Lexicon of Freemasonry," page 195)*

## CONCLUSION

Thus, it seems clear, the Hiram Abiff of Freemasonry is not an historical character and certainly not a biblical one. Rather, he actually represents Osiris, the Egyptian Sun-god; and the reenactment of the Legend of Hiram Abiff is actually the reenactment of the legend of Isis and Osiris.

Thus, each sincere man who is initiated into the Third (Master Mason) Degree of Masonry impersonates Osiris, the Sun-god of Egypt, and enters into his life of good deeds, his death, his burial and is "raised" in his resurrection from the dead. With this understood, it is then easy to understand the statement in the Kentucky Monitor (handbook for all Blue Lodge Masonry in the Grand Lodge of Kentucky) that, while the Christian's Messiah is called Jesus, the Mason's Messiah is called Hiram (Kentucky Monitor, "The Spirit of Masonry," xv).

## Footnotes

[1] *It puzzles me that no one has questioned the necessity for a "substitute" for the lost Grand Masonic Word. If it was lost at the death of Hiram because only he knew it, then why, when Hiram was raised back to life, didn't Solomon just ask him what the real, original one was? All Solomon needed to do was to say something like, "Hiram...praise the Lord that you are no longer dead! Now, what was that word all this fuss has been about?"*

[2] *I Kings 7:13-47*

[3] *I Chron. 17:1-15; 22:11-29:9 (especially 28:19)*

# THE 32ND DEGREE LECTURE

As the Masonic candidate comes into the Lodge for the first time he is told that he will be brought to the light. Then he is told that he has made a beginning toward the light but has not yet arrived. In the Second Degree light is again sought but not quite attained. He receives "additional light" but, again, it is only partial fulfillment. Then, in the Third (Master Mason) Degree, he is supposedly brought to final fulfillment. Again, he only receives "more light." Even in this climactic degree of the Master Mason where he goes through the death, burial and resurrection of Osiris the Sun-god, he is not fully enlightened. He has been given more teaching about the mysteries and their symbols, relating to the meaning of life, death and eternity. The "true light" of understanding and intellectual rebirth is still beyond his grasp... it is still up there somewhere, higher up the mountain and farther out ahead.

Then he is led to believe that the light — the real enlightenment — is to be found in the "higher degrees." In each one of these degrees beyond the Blue Lodge the seeker expects to finally reach and obtain the light. However, like the carrot on the stick, always out before the reluctant donkey to draw him onward, it remains, each time, beyond his reach. "Next time you'll reach it," the system infers each time; but the light still remains out of reach. Each time, in every higher degree, the seeking candidate doesn't quite get there. But there is always the next degree. "Surely," the candidate reasons, "... surely I will reach the light in the next degree." But he is disappointed each time.

Then comes the final degree, that terminal earned degree, the 32nd Degree. This is the top of the mountain, final fulfillment! From the very top of the Masonic Mountain one can surely see all things clearly. At the top of the mountain there should be pure air, full light and nothing hid! It has been a long and expensive climb, one that not everyone makes. At least the light will be reached there ! After all, that is the ultimate goal — the end of the line — and you can't go any higher than the top!

Alas, it is not to be. The candidate receiving the 32nd Degree is told that he has still not reached the light. He is told that he has, indeed, reached the top of the mountain, but that the mountaintop is covered with clouds and mists. The light is still obscured, still "out there somewhere" beyond him.

"Sorry, brother," the candidate is told in effect, "you will just have to press on and find the light for yourself." Here at the pinnacle of the earned degrees of Freemasonry the candidate is given his final teaching, the very last revelation in his quest for the light. Here is that lecture, verbatim, exactly as it is given to the candidates, just as Jim Shaw gave it so many times. Let's allow it to speak for itself.

## THE LECTURE OF THE 32ND DEGREE

"You are here to learn, if you can learn, and to remember what you have been taught. In the Scottish Rite you will be taught that our ancient ancestors who knew all the Mysteries left enough traces so that we today with diligent labor and teaching may renew them and bring them to light for your enlightenment. We now come to the great symbol of Pythagoras. Our symbols have descended to us from the Aryans, and many were invented by Pythagoras, who studied in Egypt and Babylon. In order to preserve the great truths learned from the profane, there were invented some of our symbols that represent the profoundest of truths descended to us from our white ancestors. Many have been lost, lost as was the true word at the death of our Grand Master Hiram Abiff.

"The ancient Masters invented some of these symbols to express the result of deity. They did not attempt to name him, but rather tried to express their reverence by describing him as Ahura-Mazda, spirit of light. They conceived the idea that Ahura had seven potencies or emanations, four of these they thought of as Male and three Female. The four male potencies of Ahura by which he governed the universe were: the divine might; the divine wisdom; the divine word; and the divine sovereignty. The three female potencies were: productiveness; health; and vitality.

"Look to the East, my brothers...and behold the seven-pointed star, the great symbol of this degree, with the seven colors of the rainbow. The seven colors and seven points represent the seven potencies of Ahura.

"Observe now the great Delta of Pythagoras consisting of 36 lights arranged in eight rows to form an equilateral triangle. The light at the apex of the Delta represents Ahura-Mazda, source of all light. This represents the seven remaining potencies of Ahura.

"The right angle triangle of three lights around the altar represents the famous 47th proposition of Euclid, or the Pythagorian theorum, which is used to conceal and reveal philosophical truths. The real significance of the cross is that of Ahura and his four male emanations, emanating from him. The four animals of the prophet Ezekiel represent these same four male emanations: Man, the divine word; the Eagle, divine wisdom; the Bull, divine might; and the Lion, divine sovereignty.

"Every equilateral triangle is a symbol of trinity, as are all groups of three in the Lodge, as the Sun, the Moon, and the Worshipful Master, in the sacred and mystic symbol AUM of the Hindus, whose origin and meaning no one here knows, the great trinity of the Aryans was symbolized by the Adepts. Among the Hindus it symbolized the supreme god of gods. The Brahmins, because of its awful and sacred meaning, hesitated to pronounce it aloud, and when doing so placed a hand in front of the mouth to deaden the sound. This triliteral name for god is composed of three Sanscrit letters. The first letter A stands for the creator (Brahma); the second letter U for (Vishnu) the preserver; the third letter M for (Siva) the destroyer. AUM it is, ineffable, not because it cannot be pronounced, but because it is pronounced A-A-A-U-U-U-M-M-M. All these things which you can learn by study, concentration, and contemplation, have come down to us from our ancient ancestors through Zaranthustra and Pythagoras.

"You have reached the mountain peak of Masonic instruction, a peak covered by a mist, which YOU in search for further light can penetrate only by your own efforts. Now we hope you will study diligently the lessons of all our degrees so that there will be nurtured within you a consuming desire to pierce the pure white light of Masonic wisdom. And before we let you go, let me give you a hint and that is all that the greatest Mystics ever give. The hint is in the Royal Secret, it is there that you may learn to find that light. Yes, brothers, the hint is in the Royal Secret. The true word-Man, born of a double nature (of what we call Good and what we call Evil; spiritual and earthly; mortal and immortal) finds the purpose of his being ONLY WHEN THESE TWO NATURES ARE IN PERFECT HARMONY.

"Harmony, my bretheren, Harmony, is the true word and the Royal Secret which makes possible the empire of true Masonic Brotherhood!"

## AND THAT'S IT !

Well, there it is. This absurd, disarticulated mixture of silly contradiction, pagan blasphemy and unfulfilled promise is all they get. They are now "Princes of the Royal Secret," and aren't even sure what the secret is! However, the most significant thing about it is, I believe, that the mountaintop they have *finally* reached is "a peak covered with mist" which they can penetrate only by their own efforts.

Here they are at the final destination, the 32nd Degree, and they find out that it isn't the final destination! In fact, they learn that not only must they press on and reach the final destination on their own, they don't even know what that destination is! After spending all this money and effort to reach "the Light," they are told they still are not there, that they must search farther and find it on their own. And they still don't really know what it is!

And these victimized men, "ever learning, and never able to come to the knowledge of the truth," don't even realize that they are victims. How very sad.

## A PRAYER FOR FREEDOM

The effects of involvement in such things as Freemasonry (and its affiliates such as Demolay, Rainbow Girls and Eastern Star) can cling to us — even to the sincere Christian — hindering, limiting and blinding. The seeds of spiritual confusion, having been sown, can put roots down deeply into our lives, bringing ongoing trouble. The resulting problems may be obvious and dramatic; or they may be so subtle as to be hardly noticed.

Whatever the situation, having once been exposed to this pagan poison with its sugar coating of "goodness," the remedy is the same: "Whosoever shall call on the name of the Lord shall be delivered" (Joel 2:32).

God will never override our wills and force us to be free. He waits, more than willing, to liberate us when we ask Him. It seems true that if we don't ask, we will go on indefinitely, carrying the doubts, fears and other problems that entered our lives through the open door of Masonic involvement. God grieves, and we suffer; yet the problems remain until we ask Him to free us.

So why not ask? Even if you're not sure you need to, what is there to lose? Just tell the Lord, out loud, that you renouce all involvement in Masonry, its branches and all other pagan , occult things, and ask Him to deliver you from all its effects and make you truly, fully and freely His child by faith in Christ Jesus. If you mean it, He will do it — not because you deserve it, but because you need it. God is not legalistic; He is infinitely gracious. You have only to ask, and mean it; He will do the rest.

If you would like a model prayer to follow, just pray this prayer:

*Heavenly Father, I want truly to be your child, and I want to be completely free. I confess that Jesus is Lord, I believe you raised Him from the dead and I confess my need of the new birth and freedom He alone can give. I want this. I renounce Freemasonry and all its affiliated groups, forms and activities, with all the paganism they represent. I renounce all things occult and pagan that have touched my life directly or come into my life through my family. I renounce it all, turn from it and ask you to forgive me, free and deliver me from all its consequences. I ask you to fill me completely with your Holy Spirit and lead me in the way I should go. I count this done, and thank you for it, in the mighty name of Jesus Christ my Lord. Amen.*

# INDEX

**159**

# More Good Books From Huntington House Publishers

*Inside the New Age Nightmare* by Randall Baer

Now, for the first time, one of the most powerful and influential leaders of the New Age movement has come out to expose the deceptions of the organization he once led. New Age magazines and articles have for many years hailed Randall Baer as their most "radically original" and "Advanced" thinker... "light years ahead of others" says leading New Age magazine *East-West Journal.* His best-selling books on quartz crystals, self-transformation, and planetary ascension have won world-wide acclaim and been extolled by New Agers from all walks of life.

Here from a New Age insider the secret plans they have spawned to take over our public, private, and political institutions. Have these plans already been implemented in your church, business, or organization? Discover the seduction of the demonic forces at work—turned from darkness to light, Randall Baer reveals the methods of the New Age movement as no one else can. Find out what you can do to stop the New Age movement from destroying our way of life.

*ISBN 0-910311-58-7 $8.95*

*The Devil's Web* by Pat Pulling with Kathy Cawthon

This explosive expose presents the first comprehensive guide to childhood and adolescent occult involvement. Written by a nationally recognized occult crime expert, the author explains how the violent occult underworld operates and how they stalk and recruit our children, teenagers and young adults for their evil purposes.The author leaves no stone unturned in her investigation and absolves no one of the responsibility of protecting our children. She dispels myths and raises new questions examining the very real possibility of the existence of major occult networks which may include members of law enforcement, government officials and other powerful individuals.

*ISBN 0-910311-59-5 $8.95 Trade paper*
*ISBN 0-910311-63-3 $16.95 Hard cover*

*From Rock to Rock* by Eric Barger

Over three years in the making, the pages of this book represent thousands of hours of detailed research as well as over twenty-six years of personal experience and study.The author presents a detailed expose on: current Rock entertainers, Rock concerts, videos, lyrics and occult symbols used within the industry. He also presents a rating system for over *fifteen hundred* past and present Rock groups and artists.

*ISBN 0-910311-61-7 $8.95*

*The Deadly Deception: Freemasonry Exposed By One Of Its Top Leaders* by Tom McKenney

Presents a frank look at Freemasonry and its origin. Learn of the "secrets" and "deceptions" that are practiced daily around the world. Find out why Masonry teaches that it is the true religion, that all other religions are but corrupted and perverted forms of Masonry.

*ISBN 0-910311-54-4 $7.95*

*Lord! Why Is My Child A Rebel?* by Jacob Aranza

This book offers an analysis of the root causes of teenage rebellion and offers practical solutions disoriented parents. Aranza focuses on the turbulent to teenage years, and how to survive those years both you and the child!Must reading for parents especially for those with strong-willed children. This book will help you avoid the traps in which many parents are caught and put you on the road to recovery with your rebel.

*ISBN 0-910311-62-5 $6.95*

*Seduction of the Innocent Revisited* by John Fulce

You honestly can't judge a book by its cover especially a comic book! Comic books of yesteryear bring to mind cute cartoon characters, super-heroes battling the forces of evil or a sleuth tracking down the bad guy clue-by-clue. But that was a long, long time ago. Today's comic books aren't innocent at all! Author John Fulce asserts that "super-heroes" are constantly found in the nude engaging in promiscuity, and satanic symbols are abundant throughout the pages. Fulce says most parents aren't aware of the contents of today's comic books—of what their children are absorbing from these seemingly innocent forms of entertainment. As a comic book collector for many years, Fulce opened his own comic book store in 1980, only to sell the business a few short years later due to the steady influx of morally unacceptable material. What's happening in the comic book industry? Fulce outlines the moral, biblical, and legal aspects, and proves his assertions with page after page of illustrations. We need to pay attention to what our children are reading, Fulce claims. Comic books are not as innocent as they used to be.

*ISBN 0-910311-66-8 $8.95*

*New World Order: The Ancient Plan of Secret Societies* by William Still

Secret societies such as Freemasons have been active since before the advent of Christ, yet most of us don't realize what they are or the impact they've had on many historical events. For example, did you know secret societies played a direct role in the French Revolutions of the 18th and 19th centuries and the Russian Revolution of the 20th century? Author William Still brings into focus the actual manipulative work of the societies, and the "Great Plan" they follow, much to the ignorance of many of those who are blindly led into the society's organizations. Their ultimate goal is simple: world dictatorship and unification of all mankind into a world confederation.

Most Masons are good, decent men who join for fellowship, but they are deceived—pulled away from their religious heritage. Only those who reach the highest level of the Masons know its true intentions. Masons and Marxists alike follow the same master. Ultimately it is a struggle between two foes the forces of religion versus the forces of anti-religion. Still asserts that although the final battle is near-at-hand, the average person has the power to thwart the efforts of secret societies. Startling and daring, this is the first successful attempt by an author to unveil the designs of secret societies from the beginning, up to the present and into the future and to educate the community on how to recognize the signals and to take the necessary steps to impede their progress.

*ISBN 0-910311-64-1 $8.95*

*Hidden Dangers of the Rainbow* by Constance Cumbey

The first to uncover and expose the New Age movement, this national #1 bestseller paved the way for all other books on the subject. It has become a giant in its category. This book provides a vivid expose of the New Age movement, which the author contends is dedicated to wiping out Christianity and establishing a one world order. This movement, a vast network of occult and pagan organizations, meets the test of prophecy concerning the Antichrist.

ISBN 0-910311-03-X $8.95

### To Grow By Storybook Readers by Janet Friend

Today quality of education is a major concern; consequently, more and more parents have turned to home schooling to teach their children how to read. The *To Grow By Storybook Readers* by Janet Friend can greatly enhance your home schooling reading program. The set of readers consists of 18 storybook readers plus 2 activity books. The *To Grow By Storybook Readers* have been designed to be used in conjunction with Marie LeDoux's PLAY 'N TALK phonic program but will work well with other orderly phonic programs.

These are the first phonic readers that subtly but positively instill scriptural moral values. They're a joy to use because no prior instructional experience is necessary. The *To Grow By Storybook Readers* allow parents and children to work together learning each sound. As your child progresses through the readers, he learns to appreciate his own ability to understand and think logically about word and sentence construction, thereby raising the self-esteem and confidence of the child.

You can lead your child step-by-step into the exciting and fun world of reading and learning, without heavy reliance on memorization. Repetition and rearrangement will leave your child begging to read page after page. Whether it's a home educational program or a phonic based program in school, these readers can substantially improve a child's reading capabilities and his desire to learn.

ISBN 0-910311-69-2 $64.95 per set

### The Delicate Balance by John Zajac

Did you know that the Apostle John and George Washington had revealed to them many of the same end-time events? It's true! Accomplished scientist, inventor, and speaker John Zajac asserts that science and religion are not opposed. He uses science to demonstrate the newly understood relevance of the Book of Revelation. Read about the catastrophic forces at work today that the ancient prophets and others foretold. You'll wonder at George Washington's description of an angelic being which appeared to him and showed him end-time events that were to come—the accuracy of Nostradamus (who converted to Christianity) and the warnings of St. John that are revealed in the Book of Revelation—earthquakes, floods, terrorism—what does it all mean? No other author has examined these topics from Zajac's unique perspective or presented such a reasonable and concise picture of the whole.

ISBN 0-910311-57-9 $8.95

### Backward Masking Unmasked by Jacob Aranza

Rock music affects millions of young people and adults with lyrics exalting drugs, Satan, violence and immorality. But there is even a more sinister threat: hidden messages that exalt the Prince of Darkness!

ISBN 0-910311-04-8 $6.95

Also on cassette tape! Hear authentic demonic backward masking from rock music.

ISBN 0-910311-23-4 $6.95

***Personalities in Power: The Making of Great Leaders*** byFlorence Littauer

You'll laugh and cry as Florence Littauer shares with you heart-warming accounts of the personal lives of some of our greatest leaders. Learn of their triumphs and tragedies, and become aware of the different personality patterns that exist and how our leaders have been influenced by them.Discover your own strengths and weaknesses by completing the Personality Chart included in this book. *Personalities in Power* lets you understand yourself and others and helps you live up to your full potential.

*ISBN 0-910311-56-0 $8.95*

***The Last Days Collection*** by Last Days Ministries

Heart-stirring, faith-challenging messages from Keith Green, David Wilkerson, Melody Green, Leonard Ravenhill, Winkie Pratney, Charles Finney and William Booth are designed to awaken complacent Christians to action.

*ISBN 0-910311-42-0 $8.95*

***The Lucifer Connection*** by Joseph Carr

Shirley MacLaine and other celebrities are persuading millions that the New Age movement can fill the spiritual emptiness in their lonely lives. Joseph Carr explains why the New Age movement is the most significant and potentially destructive challenge to the church today. But is it new? How should Christians protect themselves and their children from this insidious threat? This book is a prophetic, information-packed examination by one of the most informed authors in America.

*ISBN 0-910311-42-0 $7.95*

***Exposing the Aids Scandal: What You Don't Know Can Kill You*** by Dr. Paul Cameron

Where do you turn when those who control the flow of information in this country withhold the truth? Why is the national media hiding facts from the public? Can Aids be spread in ways we're not being told? Finally a book that gives you a total account of the AIDS epidemic, and what steps can be taken to protect yourself. What you don't know can kill you!

*ISBN 0-910311-52-8 $7.95*

***A Reasonable Reason to Wait*** by Jacob Aranza

God speaks specifically about premarital sex. Aranza provides a definite, frank discussion on premarital sex. He also provides a biblical healing message to those who have already been sexually involved before marriage. This book delivers an important message to young people, as well as their parents.

*ISBN 0-910311-21-8 $5.95*

***Jubilee on Wall Street*** by David Knox Barker

On October 19, 1987, the New York Stock Exchange suffered its greatest loss in history—twice that of the 1929 crash. Will this precipitate a new Great Depression? This riveting book is a look at what the author believes is the inevitable collapse of the world's economy. Using the biblical principle of the Year of Jubilee, a refreshing dose of optimism and an easy-to-read style, the author shows readers how to avoid economic devastation.

*ISBN 0-933-451-03-2 $7.95*

*America Betrayed* by Marlin Maddoux

This hard-hitting book exposes the forces in our country which seek to destroy the family, the schools and our values. This book details exactly how the news media manipulates your mind. Marlin Maddoux is the host of the popular, national radio talk show "Point of View."

*ISBN 0-910311-18-8 $6.95*

*Dinosaurs and the Bible* by David W. Unfred

Every reader, young and old, will be fascinated by this ever-mysterious topic—exactly what happened to the dinosaurs? Author David Unfred draws a very descriptive picture of the history and fate of the dinosaurs on Earth, using the Bible as a reference guide.

In this educational and informative book, Unfred answers such questions as: Did dinosaurs really exist? Does the Bible mention dinosaurs? What happened to dinosaurs, or are there some still living awaiting discovery? Unfred uses the Bible to help unlock the ancient mysteries of the lumbering creatures, and teaches how those mysteries can educate us about God the Creator and our God of Love.

*ISBN 0-910311-70-6 $12.95 Hardcover*

*"Soft Porn" Plays Hardball* by Dr. Judith Reisman

With amazing clarity, the author demonstrates that pornography imposes on society a view of women and children that encourages violence and sexual abuse. As crimes against women and children increase to alarming proportions, it's of paramount importance that we recognize the cause of this violence. Pornography should be held accountable for the havoc it has wreaked in our homes and our country.

*ISBN 0-901311-65-X  $ 8.95 Trade paper*
*ISBN 0-910311-92-7 $16.95  Hardcover*

*Devil Take the Youngest* by Winkie Pratney

A history of Satan's hatred of innocence and his historical treachery against the young. Pratney begins his journey in ancient Babylon and continues through to modern-day America where infants are murdered daily and children are increasingly victimized through pornography, prostitution and humanism.

*ISBN 0-910311-29-3 $8.95*

*God's Rebels* by Henry Lee Curry III

From his unique perspective Dr. Henry Lee Curry III offers a fascinating look at the lives of some of our greatest Southern religious leaders during the Civil War. The rampant Evangelical Christianity prominent at the outbreak of the Civil War, asserts Dr. Curry, is directly traceable to the 2nd Great Awakening of the early 1800s. The evangelical tradition, with its emphasis on strict morality, individual salvation, and emotional worship, had influenced most of Southern Protestantism by this time. Southerners unquestionably believed the voice of the ministers to be the voice of God ; consequently, the church became one of the most powerful forces influencing Confederate life and morale. Inclined toward a Calvinistic emphasis on predestination, the South was confident that God would sustain its way of life.

Dr. Curry illuminates the many different activities in which Confederate clergymen engaged. He focuses on three prominent clergymen in the heart of the South:. James A. Duncan, editor of the Richmond Christian Advocate; Moses I. Hoge, Honorary chaplain of the Confederate Congress who ran the Union blockade in order to get Bibles for Confederate soldiers; and Charles F. E. Minnigerods, a pastor of one of the most important parishes in the South.

Dr. Curry is a Virginian. He holds degrees from the University of Virginia, Duke University, and Emory University. While teaching at Mercer University's Atlanta Campus, his course on The Civil War and Reconstruction was always very popular.

ISBN:   0-910311-67-6 *Trade pape r$12.95*
ISBN:  0-910311-68-4 *Hard cover $21.95*

# Order These Books from Huntington House Publishers!

____America Betrayed—Marlin Maddoux. . . . . . . . . . . . . $ 6.95 _____

____Backward Masking Unmasked—Jacob Aranza. . . . . . 6.95 _____

____Deadly Deception: Freemasonry—Tom McKenney. . . 7.95 _____

____Delicate Balance—John Zajac. . . . . . . . . . . . . . . . . . . 8.95 _____

____Devil Take The Youngest—Winkey Pratney. . . . . . . . 8.95 _____

____The Devils Web—Pat Pulling with Kathy Cawthon. . . . . . . . .

trade paper. . 8.95 _____

hard cover. . .16.95 _____

____*Dinosaurs and the Bible—Dave Unfred. . . . . . . . . . . 12.95 _____

____Exposing the AIDS Scandal—Dr. Paul Cameron. . . . . . 7.95 _____

____*From Rock to Rock—Eric Barger. . . . . . . . . . . . . . . . 8.95 _____

____*God's Rebels—Henry Lee Curry III, Ph.D.. . . . . . . . . .

trade paper. .12.95 _____

hard cover. . 21.95 _____

____The Hidden Dangers of the Rainbow—

Constance Cumbey. . . . 8.95 _____

____Inside the New Age Nightmare—Randall Baer. . . . . . . 8.95 _____

____Jubilee on Wall Street—David Knox Barker. . . . . . . . 7.95 _____

____Last Days Collection—Last Days Ministries. . . . . . . . 8.95 _____

____*Lord! Why Is My Child A Rebel?—Jacob Aranza. . . . 6.95 _____

____Lucifer Connection—Joseph Carr. . . . . . . . . . . . . . . . 7.95 _____

____*New World Order: The Ancient Plan of Secret

Societies—William T. Still. . . . 8.95 _____

____Personalities in Power—Florence Littauer. . . . . . . . . . 8.95 _____

____A Reasonable Reason To Wait—Jacob Aranza. . . . . . . 5.95 _____

____*Seduction of The Innocent Revisited—John Fulce. . . . 8.95 _____

____*Soft Porn Plays Hardball—Dr. Judith A. Reisman. . . .

trade paper. . 8.95 _____

hard cover. . .16.95 _____

____*To Grow By Storybook Readers—Janet Friend. . 64.95 per set_____

Shipping and Handling _____

TOTAL _____

*New Titles

AVAILABLE AT BOOKSTORES EVERYWHERE or order direct from:
Huntington House Publishers, P.O. Box 53788, Lafayette, LA 70505

Send check/money order. For faster service use
VISA/MASTERCARD, call toll-free 1-800-749-4009
Add: Freight and handling, $2.00 for the first book ordered, and $.50 for each
additional book.

Enclosed is $_____ including postage.
Card type:
VISA/Mastercard#_____ Exp. Date_____
Name_____
Address_____
City, State, Zip_____